BEYOND THE CALL

Beyond the Call

A First Responder's Guide to Unbreakable Well-Being

DENNIS J. CARRADIN, JR.

DJC Productions

Copyright © 2024 by Dennis J. Carradin, Jr.

All rights reserved. No part of this book may be reproduced in any manner whatsoever without written permission except in the case of brief quotations embodied in critical articles and reviews.

First Printing, 2024

Dedication

To my beloved children, Denny, Melina, and Deanna,

You are the radiant stars illuminating my life's canvas, casting a glow of warmth, joy, and boundless love. This book is dedicated to you, my greatest treasures, my eternal muses, and the unwavering sources of inspiration that propel me to be a better person every day.

Denny, with your unwavering determination and contagious laughter, you light the path with resilience and courage. Melina, your kindness and compassion create empathy, reminding me of the beauty in simple acts of love. Deanna, your zest for life and infectious enthusiasm infuse each day with adventure and discovery.

Together, you form the tapestry of my heart, weaving threads of laughter, shared dreams, and unbreakable bonds. Through every challenge and triumph, you are my guiding star, illuminating the path toward becoming the best version of myself.

May this book stand as a testament to the love that fills my heart because of you. You are my greatest masterpiece, and I dedicate these pages to the three lights of my life.

With all my love,
Dad

CONTENTS

| 1 |

Preface

In the aftermath of an incident involving a police officer discharging their weapon, a profound and palpable silence settles over the police station. This atmosphere, imbued with gravity and reflection, goes beyond the absence of sound; it becomes a sacred pause, pregnant with unspoken emotions and a collective holding of breath. It's a moment where the air seems to thicken with the weight of contemplation and concern, akin to the solemnity of a church, where each footstep on the floor echoes in the prevailing quiet.

The gravity of the situation is evident in the shared gazes of colleagues, their faces etched with long, mournful expressions that communicate volumes silently. These glances, laden with empathy and shared anxiety, converge on the officer involved. The unspoken concern weaves an intricate tapestry of emotions, creating an environment where the event's ramifications are deeply felt.

In these moments, the refrain "Happy to see you, but not under these circumstances," echoes in my mind. It encapsulates a mix of relief and sorrow, highlighting the paradox of encountering a fellow officer in the wake of a critical incident. This refrain serves as a reminder of the dual nature of camaraderie in law enforcement, where the joy of reunion is overshadowed by the weight of the circumstances.

I am Dennis Carradin, and a substantial part of my career has been as a trauma therapist, deeply engaged with individuals in the law enforcement community. My journey has taken me through the realms of trauma, offering support to those who bear the badge's weight. These interactions have allowed me to witness the remarkable resilience within the human spirit.

This book, "Beyond the Call: A First Responder's Guide to Unbreakable Well-Being," is the culmination of my experiences and insights. It serves as a repository for untold narratives behind the uniform and a call to action. It seeks to illuminate the mental health struggles faced by first responders, aiming to dismantle the stigma around their psychological challenges and invite broader societal understanding and empathy.

Unveiling the Human Behind the Badge

Stepping into the police station in the aftermath of an officer-involved shooting immerses me into the raw, unfiltered emotional aftermath endured by law enforcement officers. As a trauma therapist, I serve as a silent guide, navigating the turbulent aftermath of post-traumatic stress that engulfs those sworn to protect and serve. This journey begins with the Crisis Intervention Stage, where on-scene trauma therapists like myself provide immediate support and education, recognizing the shared humanity of officers amidst the chaos.

The subsequent debriefing is a therapeutic ritual, a deep exploration of the harrowing incident when an officer had to return gunfire on an assailant. In these sessions, officers have the space to process the trauma they witnessed and experienced. The badge, often seen as a shield, momentarily reveals the vulnerable person underneath.

This step, essential for emotional healing, acknowledges the emotional weight carried by law enforcement personnel, going beyond their stoic exterior.

Short-term therapy emerges as a vital lifeline, focusing on practical, solution-oriented approaches to manage daily functioning and alleviate burgeoning post-traumatic stress. In these sessions, my aim is to bridge the gap between the badge and the person wearing it, creating an environment where officers can confront the psychological toll of their profession without fear of judgment.

Officer-involved shootings, though statistically rare, resonate deeply in the lives and careers of those dedicated to community safety. It is imperative to dismantle the myth of emotionless automatons and to see officers as complex individuals with families, hopes, and vulnerabilities. My dedication as a trauma therapist extends beyond professional obligation; it arises from countless hours spent assisting officers in the aftermath, advocating against the trivialization of their experiences for social or political purposes.

In the pages of this book, I aim to peel back the layers shrouding the often-unseen struggles of first responders. It is a deliberate effort to connect the dots between the external pressures they face and the empathy they rightfully deserve. Through these narratives, the hope is to lift the veil on the emotional intricacies of law enforcement, calling for their well-being, understanding, and support.

A Trooper's Desperate Stop

Driving on the familiar stretch of I-95, known for lurking State Troopers enforcing speed limits, I adjusted my speed to meticulous conformity. The tension of the road was broken as the flashing lights of a State Trooper pulled up behind me, signaling me to pull over.

Despite knowing I wasn't speeding, a pang of guilt, perhaps rooted in Italian Catholic guilt, still coursed through me.

As I turned on my hazard lights and placed my hands on the wheel, the young Trooper approached my vehicle with an unusual urgency. "Are you Dennis Carradin?" he asked, an unconventional start to a routine traffic stop. Confirming my identity, I was taken aback when he confessed, "I desperately need to make an appointment with you. I was nervous to call you, but I saw your vehicle and decided to stop you.".

At that moment, it became clear that this encounter was more than a routine traffic stop. The Trooper, entrusted with upholding the law, found himself in need of assistance, and he took an unconventional route to seek it. The urgency in his voice conveyed the seriousness of the situation, and I knew I had to help. It was a poignant reminder that even those tasked with maintaining order and composure can find themselves vulnerable and in need of support.

The stretch of I-95 that witnessed the unusual road stop now symbolizes the unexpected intersections of vulnerability and strength within the first responder community. The young Trooper's decision to seek help in an unconventional way speaks volumes about the prevailing stigma surrounding mental health care.

In that moment, I recognized the gravity of the situation. A Trooper, armed with authority and training, was confronting his battles, and the urgency in his voice echoed the silent struggles of many first responders. This incident underscored the need for a shift in our collective perception — a call to action to destigmatize seeking help, and to recognize that vulnerability is not a flaw but a shared human experience.

These stories are not isolated incidents but reflections of a larger truth – that the mental well- being of our first responders is a critical aspect of the societal fabric. This book delves into the heart of the matter, unraveling the intricacies of mental health care for those who dedicate their lives to answering the call, and it is my sincere hope that it serves as a guiding light toward unbreakable well-being beyond the call.

This book delves deeper into the intricate tapestry of mental health treatment for first responders. It explores the nuanced landscape of therapeutic modalities, recognizing that a one-size-fits-all approach is insufficient. Cognitive-behavioral therapy, eye movement desensitization and reprocessing (EMDR), and mindfulness-based interventions are just a few tools in the arsenal, each uniquely suited to address the diverse needs of those who stand between society and chaos.

The pages that follow are an exploration of the intersection between trauma, resilience, and mental well-being. It is an invitation to delve into the complexities of first responders' experiences and to understand the toll their duty takes on their minds and spirits. More importantly, it is a guide — a roadmap towards unbreakable well-being beyond the call.

As you embark on this journey through the heart of first responders' mental health, I urge you to shed preconceived notions and open your hearts to the realities faced by those who dedicate their lives to our safety. Let this book be a catalyst for change, a beacon illuminating the path towards a future where seeking help is not a sign of weakness, but a testament to the unyielding strength that resides in the heart of every first responder. Together, let us go beyond the call, weaving a tapestry of well-being that recognizes, honors, and uplifts those who answer the call.

| 2 |

Chapter 1: Exploring Mental Health Therapy Options for First Responders with Traumatic Reactions and Posttraumatic Stress Disorder PTSD.

Introduction

Chapter 1 delves deep into the complex world of mental health therapy for first responders struggling with trauma reactions and post-traumatic stress disorder (PTSD). It offers insight into the unique challenges faced by these unheralded heroes - police officers, paramedics, firefighters, and EMTs - who navigate a treacherous environment where constant exposure to traumatizing events takes its toll on their psychological well-being. This chapter explores their experiences, examining the emotional and psychological ramifications. We dissect their traumatic reactions, providing insight into the intricate nature of PTSD. The narrative progresses to an in-depth examination of various therapeutic interventions designed to treat PTSD symptoms. Our aim is to identify effective therapeutic strategies to lessen the psychological strain on these heroic community defenders.

Understanding Traumatic Reactions

First responders frequently encounter life-threatening emergencies, placing them at increased risk for emotional and psychological trauma. Unaddressed, these experiences can lead to intrusive thoughts, disturbing nightmares, elevated arousal levels, or emotional numbing. If these reactions are neglected, they can become detrimental, potentially developing into full- fledged posttraumatic stress disorder (PTSD) or psychosis. Therefore, swift and tailored therapeutic interventions are necessary to reduce further suffering and prevent the progression of these conditions. Specialized interventions offer comprehensive support, equipping first responders with the necessary tools for healing from their demanding professional experiences.

Mental Health Therapy for First Responders

Mental health therapy has emerged as an essential and tailored response to the unique challenges first responders encounter following traumatic incidents, providing a comfortable space wherein traumatic experiences can be unraveled and fully processed. Going beyond immediate aftermath effects, therapy for first responders aims to address deeper layers of underlying mental health concerns brought up by their profession and its demands.

Mental health therapy for first responders goes beyond traditional counseling paradigms and explores evidence-based practices to maximize effectiveness. Cognitive-behavioral therapy (CBT) and eye movement desensitization and reprocessing (EMDR) are widely employed methods by therapists in this context. These research-backed practices provide essential guidance for first responders navigating through the often-overwhelming array of emotional states associated with trauma-inducing experiences. CBT, with its focus on altering thought patterns and behavior, helps dismantle maladaptive coping mechanisms developed because of repeated exposure to trauma events. Meanwhile, EMDR helps mitigate impact while building resilience through bilateral stimulation, serving to mitigate its impact and develop resilience.

Mental health therapy for first responders recognizes the intimate link between physical and psychological well-being. Therapists use collaborative efforts with individuals to address trauma-related symptoms as well as work together on creating effective coping mechanisms. By creating an open and vulnerable space, therapists enable first responders to confront and process their traumatic experiences, leading them to healing and psychological resilience - thus becoming an invaluable resource in helping first responders navigate post-traumatic stress and its myriad implications on their overall well-being.

Approaches for Different First Responder Groups

Each subgroup of first responders faces its own set of stressors and triggers, necessitating individualized therapeutic solutions tailored to the specific challenges they experience. Police officers may require therapy tailored specifically for law enforcement officers to manage constant exposure to violence while meeting increased workload demands; on the other hand, firefighters often experience emotional trauma from responding to fires that result in loss of life and property damage that necessitate interventions focused on providing comfort and healing.

Paramedics and EMTs who provide emergency services frequently face life-or-death decisions on an everyday basis. Therefore, tailored therapeutic interventions for this subgroup are especially vital; providing them with tools to cope with both their work-related stressors and the emotional impacts of making life-altering choices in service of duty.

Dispatchers and 911 operators often face distressing calls and situations that require immediate responses, making therapy designed to relieve emotional strain a necessity for these professionals. By understanding the needs of each subgroup of first responders, mental health specialists can play a pivotal role in cultivating resilience, healing, and overall well-being among those dedicated to public safety.

Conclusion

Traumatic experiences experienced by first responders demonstrate the urgent need for specialized mental health therapy services designed to treat posttraumatic reactions and posttraumatic stress disorder (PTSD). Heal the Heroes therapy sessions are an indispensable asset in effectively meeting these challenges and building resilience within communities served by these courageous professionals. In this investigation, we explore more closely the unique challenges experienced by police officers, firefighters, paramedics, and dispatchers, while acknowledging their immense impactful roles. Advocates for targeted support take center stage, emphasizing the pivotal role that therapy sessions like Heal the Heroes play in mitigating posttraumatic reactions and restoring overall well-being. Heal the Heroes stands as an icon, providing vital mental health therapy services designed specifically to meet the unique needs of first responders. Through successful interventions and restoration of mental well-being, therapy sessions contribute to individual healing and strengthen community resilience. Heal the Heroes therapy sessions are key in building resilience within communities served by these professional providers, by acknowledging, addressing, and successfully managing posttraumatic reactions. This chapter emphasizes the indisputable significance and impact of mental health interventions such as Heal the Heroes in society at large. They serve to support those who bravely face trauma as part of their duties without seeking assistance themselves.

Recognizing Signs and Symptoms of Posttraumatic Stress Disorder

Introduction

Identification and treatment of posttraumatic stress disorder (PTSD) symptoms among first responders are essential, given their high exposure to traumatizing events. The demanding nature of their roles puts them at an increased risk of PTSD. This chapter explores the unique challenges faced by first responders such as police officers, firefighters, and emergency medical personnel who frequently encounter distressing situations with long-lasting psychological effects.

Mental health therapy for first responders struggling with trauma reactions and PTSD requires careful consideration of their unique stressors and how they manifest as symptoms. Early detection is key in managing mental health effectively, necessitating exploration of all associated signs and symptoms unique to the first responder experience.

This discourse guides through the complex terrain of mental health support for first responders, providing insight into their unique challenges. By detailing signs and symptoms associated with PTSD, this dialogue serves as a guide for both first responders and their caretakers. Furthermore, it emphasizes the necessity of creating an environment conducive to swift access to tailored mental health therapy and support services, meeting immediate needs and contributing to the broader discussion on improving public safety.

Primary Signs of Posttraumatic Stress Disorder

PTSD in First Responders is a complex issue, often manifesting through symptoms that go beyond simply recalling traumatic experiences. These individuals who bravely navigate intense, often life-threatening situations may find themselves experiencing nightmares, intrusive thoughts, and vivid flashbacks that recreate what has transpired in their past lives. These manifestations go well beyond mere memories; they elicit emotional and sensory responses that pervade everyday life, creating havoc in relationships and employment opportunities. The effects become overwhelming. Relationships may become compromised when burdened by emotional turmoil, while employment may present new obstacles as the mental and emotional stress caused by trauma impairs daily tasks. Thus, treating First Responders suffering from post- traumatic stress disorder requires an in-depth knowledge of its subtleties; treatment should aim not only at relieving the immediate symptoms but also at creating balance in all areas of their life.

Avoidance as a Coping Mechanism in PTSD

Individuals suffering from PTSD, especially First Responders, frequently rely on avoidance as a coping strategy to cope with profoundly disturbing experiences. This strategy involves a deliberate and conscious effort to avoid places, individuals, and activities associated with the traumatizing event. Such efforts are aimed at protecting oneself emotionally from potentially distressful memories or triggers resurfacing from its aftermath. Deliberate avoidance can eventually become so ingrained that discussing events leading to emotional trauma becomes taboo territory. As a result, individuals often struggle with communicating the extent of their emotional turmoil to loved ones.

In the long term, avoidance has far-reaching repercussions that extend beyond straining interpersonal relationships. It can impact once enjoyable activities that gradually lose their appeal, leading to an intense sense of isolation as the individual disengages both from traumatic memories and from supportive networks that could assist in their healing journey. Mental health therapy for First Responders with traumatic reactions and PTSD must address these complex layers of avoidance and its repercussions to facilitate healing and recovery. Interventions should focus on breaking the cycle of avoidance, encouraging open dialogue, and rebuilding connections. These steps are integral in the process of healing and recovery.

Cognitive and Mood Shifts

PTSD can have a devastating impact on the mental well-being of First Responders, manifesting through emotions and cognition that are out of sync. Within this web of symptoms, intricate systems emerge - including negative thought patterns, self-blame, and persistent feelings of guilt - each contributing to the other. This mental distress weaves an altered perception of reality, leading to a range of negative emotions such as hopelessness, depression, and anxiety. The psychological issues associated with PTSD extend beyond emotions, also impacting cognitive processes. These issues can include concentration problems, memory lapses, and altered sleeping patterns. As First Responders navigate high-stakes situations that are increasingly complex, any additional cognitive burdens can compound trauma reactions and make life even more challenging for them. Therefore, effectively meeting the mental health challenges of First Responders requires an individualized approach that addresses both their complex emotions and cognitive obstacles induced by PTSD.

Physical Consequences of Trauma

Addressing the mental health needs of First Responders struggling with PTSD requires exploring both physical and emotional manifestations. PTSD is a complex psychological condition that not only manifests through emotional upheavals but leaves indelible scars on the body itself. Physical symptoms like persistent headaches, stomachaches, muscle tension, or an increased heart rate serve as tangible evidence of the profound impact of trauma.

The physical ramifications of trauma extend far beyond simple discomfort. They manifest in behavioral responses such as an excessive startle response, elevated anxiety levels, and hypersensitivity to loud noises or sudden movements. These reactions demonstrate the profound relationship between mental and physical well-being in First Responder contexts.

Recognizing these signs and symptoms is the cornerstone of mental health therapy for First Responders. It involves understanding how trauma affects both the mind and body in its entirety. Seeking assistance should not be viewed as a sign of weakness; rather, it represents courage and resilience. Accepting help is an essential part of recovery, signifying an effort to restore emotional and mental stability and improve overall well-being. Psychotherapy is an invaluable resource for First Responders. It helps them navigate the complex terrain of trauma, build resilience, and facilitate healing.

Mental Health Therapy and First Responders.

Introduction

Mental health therapy often goes underappreciated in first responder medicine. However, its significance cannot be understated regarding traumatic reactions and post-traumatic stress disorder (PTSD) among first responders. This segment explores the immense impact mental health therapy has on first responders such as police officers, 911 dispatchers, firefighters, paramedics, and EMTs. It's essential to not only acknowledge the existence of mental health therapy, but also recognize it as a key component of personalized well-being plans, tailored to the specific challenges faced by first responders.

Mental health therapy is an invaluable ally for professionals operating in high-stress environments and exposed to traumatizing events. Psychological support is vitally important for them in processing and managing the emotional fallout from these experiences. Evidence-based treatments are targeted specifically toward trauma, stress relief, and the unique challenges inherent to being a first responder.

As mental health therapy within the first responder community is inherently collaborative, we must emphasize its collaborative nature. Police officers, 911 dispatchers, firefighters, paramedics, and EMTs occupy closely intertwined roles. By acknowledging these shared experiences and challenges, mental health specialists can tailor therapeutic approaches to meet the specific needs and dynamics of first responder teams.

Mental health therapy extends beyond an individual first responder to address the collective well-being of an entire team. Mental health care creates a healthier and more resilient response system. Additionally, therapy is an important preventative measure against trauma, mitigating its impacts on first responders' mental well-being.

Mental health therapy for first responders is more than just a part of well-being care plans; it's integral to building mental resilience and overall health among those who dedicate themselves to public safety. Recognizing, appreciating, and investing in mental health therapy is not simply individual responsibility; it is essential for fostering resilient and mentally healthy first responder communities.

Understanding Traumatic Reactions and Post Traumatic Stress Disorder

First responders often face challenging and emotionally draining experiences during their service, which can profoundly alter their well-being. These incidents often leave lasting repercussions, such as crippling anxiety, pervasive depression, overwhelming anger, or debilitating insomnia. Attaining equilibrium for first responders often comes at the price of their mental well-being, making the addressing of mental health therapy an invaluable way of returning them to equilibrium.

Mental health therapy stands as an invaluable support system for those facing trauma-induced reactions or post-traumatic stress disorder (PTSD). Therapy provides an essential service in navigating the intricacies of trauma by engaging with the emotional and psychological responses of individuals. Counseling offers not only an environment to process events that have left an indelible mark but also equips first responders with tools for dealing with their emotional landscape.

Therapeutic interventions, designed specifically to meet the unique challenges faced by first responders, allow individuals to regain control over their lives. They build resilience and enable them to handle daily responsibilities with greater freedom and emotional stability. Mental health therapy, as an integral component of first responder health, underscores the significance of providing proactive and targeted support systems in mitigating any potential long-term consequences of their service.

Custom Designed Therapy Program for Police Officers.

First responders, particularly police officers, face unique stressors from being exposed to violence on an ongoing basis and their overwhelming responsibility of maintaining public safety. These stressors can lead to trauma reactions or post-traumatic stress disorder (PTSD), making specialized mental health therapy a necessity within law enforcement communities. Such therapy explores the psychological costs exacted by their profession and offers tailored approaches for meeting the unique challenges faced by first responders.

Mental health therapy designed specifically for police officers transcends conventional interventions by recognizing and targeting issues common in law enforcement. Interventions go beyond talk therapy alone and may include multiple approaches. Coping mechanisms tailored for their unique stressors become the focus, to equip officers with resilient strategies for the inherent challenges of the law enforcement profession. Specifically tailored coping mechanisms may help boost emotional well-being in times of adversity and ensure resilience is instilled throughout.

Communication skills, key in law enforcement environments, also play a vital role in therapeutic interventions. Police officers frequently face situations that demand precise and effective communication, and therapy can help refine this skill set. By honing these abilities further, officers can gain the strength to deal with high-pressure scenarios more easily while creating deeper connections among themselves and with the communities they serve.

Mental health therapy for first responders entails addressing specific difficulties encountered on the job, from processing traumatic incidents to managing complex emotions associated with their profession. Therapists collaborate closely with officers to overcome these challenges, creating an open and accepting atmosphere where officers can address and acknowledge the emotional costs of their profession.

Mental health therapy for first responders, particularly police officers, goes far beyond generic approaches. It acknowledges the unique stressors inherent to their profession and develops tailored interventions to increase resilience against burnout. By diving deeply into their experiences and understanding them as individuals, specialized therapy becomes an invaluable way of safeguarding mental well-being among those devoted to protecting public safety.

Support for Firefighters

Firefighting presents First Responders with unique psychological stresses that go far beyond physical danger, often leading to post-traumatic stress disorder (PTSD). Due to its multidimensional nature, mental health therapy for firefighters must be tailored specifically to address more than the immediate psychological aftermath of traumatizing events; an effective therapy regime for First Responders must encompass intricate facets of their well-being.

At its core, mental health therapy for firefighters must encompass more than crisis intervention. It should be an ongoing initiative focused on creating long-term resilience and mitigating cumulative trauma exposure. Stress management techniques are central, providing firefighters with tools to navigate high-pressure scenarios intrinsic to their profession. Resilience-building exercises help individuals recover quickly from setbacks while building mental toughness.

Mental health therapy for first responders must consider the challenges posed by repeat exposure to trauma. Recognizing and responding to its long-term impacts are essential in maintaining sustained well-being. Therapeutic interventions must offer supportive environments where firefighters can process and integrate cumulative trauma, encouraging healing and warding off potential PTSD symptoms.

By improving mental resilience, tailored therapy not only safeguards individual well-being but also enhances community service effectiveness. An empowered firefighter, adept at navigating complex roles, responding quickly in emergencies, and contributing meaningfully to community well-being, is better equipped to serve.

Mental health therapy for firefighters transcends mere coping strategies; it becomes a key component of their professional growth, providing emotional protection against the unique challenges of their line of duty. Comprehensive and tailored therapy approaches enable firefighters to manage immediate trauma-induced reactions and build long-term psychological well-being, fostering both individual resilience and community service efficacy.

Nurturing Paramedics and EMTs

Paramedics and emergency medical technicians (EMTs) often find themselves in intense, life- threatening situations, leading them to develop trauma reactions and PTSD. These dedicated first responders must grapple with the emotional toll of their profession, necessitating special mental health therapy approaches tailored specifically for them. A comprehensive strategy should consider both their daily experiences and any symptoms of trauma they might be suffering from.

Psychotherapy for first responders must recognize their important role in protecting others. Stress reduction must become an imperative due to constant exposure to high-stakes scenarios. Furthermore, therapeutic processes should emphasize cultivating and strengthening coping mechanisms tailored specifically to their profession's demands - this involves not only dealing with posttraumatic events but also offering tools to manage ongoing challenges related to work life.

Mental health therapy for paramedics and EMTs should aim to ease emotional strain without diminishing the quality of care delivered. Therapists must assist these first responders in understanding and managing the emotional burdens they carry while cultivating self-awareness and emotional resilience, to help navigate the complexities of their profession while upholding high standards of service delivery.

Recognizing the significance of emotional well-being for emergency medical services providers is of vital importance. A holistic approach to mental health therapy for paramedics and EMTs recognizes both immediate trauma effects as well as long-term effects on mental well-being. By offering targeted interventions that foster self-care, stress reduction techniques, coping skills development, and targeted therapy sessions for first responders devoted to saving others, mental health professionals can create an enabling environment in which first responders can manage challenges faced in their profession while continuing to deliver services of the highest caliber.

Conclusion

First responders struggling with trauma reactions and post-traumatic stress disorder (PTSD) will find mental health therapy an invaluable ally in managing their emotional well-being. Police officers, firefighters, paramedics, EMTs, and dispatchers - often exposed to challenging situations that leave lasting emotional scars - can find essential relief in mental health therapy.

Therapy offers more than immediate comfort; it provides an interactive space where emotions can be explored and processed. The unique challenges faced by first responders necessitate specific interventions tailored to their experiences. Therapy offers a setting to distill, examine, and transform the raw emotions resulting from emergency response work into practical coping strategies. These strategies equip first responders with the psychological tools necessary for navigating their demanding profession.

Mental health therapy serves as an invaluable defense mechanism against posttraumatic stress disorder (PTSD). By creating a safe environment where first responders can promptly process traumas before they evolve into debilitating conditions, therapy acts as both a reactive and preventive measure. This approach helps minimize the long-term consequences associated with repeated exposure to trauma.

Mental health therapy is a vital component of any first responder's toolkit, providing both unwavering support and renewable resources to maintain resilience during crises. It replenishes mental well-being and should not be viewed as an indulgence but as an essential aspect of ensuring public safety. As society increasingly recognizes the contributions of first responders, prioritizing mental health therapy for them becomes even more important. This ensures they are well-prepared to face external crises and the internal battles that may arise from their dedicated service.

| 3 |

Chapter 2: Mental Health Therapy Approaches for First Responders

First responder minds can be an intricate web of sounds and images, necessitating an approach tailored to them in terms of compassion. "Mental Health Therapy Approaches for First Responders" takes a deliberate step into this realm of healing by exploring transformative methods specifically tailored for frontline crisis responders. With its arsenal of tools designed to address specific difficulties faced by our resilient heroes, this exploration opens doors towards recovery with thoughtful methods tailored for the unique challenges of frontline crisis responders.

Cognitive behavioral therapy (CBT) for traumatic reactions provides a structured framework to unravel the tangled web of thoughts and emotions caused by exposure to trauma. By scrutinizing cognitive patterns and altering them accordingly, CBT empowers first responders toward resilience and emotional wellness.

Eye movement desensitization and reprocessing (EMDR) therapy has quickly emerged as a transformative healing approach, unlocking potential through bilateral stimulation. Engaging in rhythmic eye movements, individuals process traumatic memories while shifting their narrative toward strength and recovery.

Exposure therapy for PTSD exemplifies the power of facing fear head-on. First responders in Exposure Therapy begin a journey toward desensitization and regaining safety by confronting their trauma in a safe setting.

Group therapy and support networks for first responders provide essential communal strength. Sharing experiences and healing together, individuals find comfort in not being alone in their struggles or triumphs.

Critical incident stress management (CISM) and critical incident response (CIR) serve as essential tools in the aftermath of crisis exposure, helping individuals manage the immediate psychological repercussions of critical incidents as well as foster long-term emotional resilience and recovery.

Exploring these therapeutic methodologies sheds light on the pathway toward mental well- being. Together, they form an extensive toolkit for the multidimensional healing of those devoted to protecting and serving - our first responders. Through understanding, support, and intentional intervention, we aim to guide them toward futures marked by profound and lasting resilience.

Cognitive Behavioral Therapy (CBT) for Traumatic Reactions

First responders often navigate daunting environments, placing them at risk for traumatized reactions and post-traumatic stress disorder (PTSD). These courageous individuals face challenges that can significantly impact their mental well-being. Amid these challenges, cognitive behavioral therapy (CBT) offers hope, tailored specifically for first responders dealing with trauma or PTSD.

CBT stands out as a therapeutic paradigm that delves into the interplay between thoughts, emotions, and behaviors. It aims not just at symptom relief but at identifying and modifying detrimental cognitive patterns and behaviors causing emotional distress. Directly addressing these cognitive processes, CBT enables individuals to develop healthier coping mechanisms and regain life control.

For first responders, CBT offers an effective way to handle trauma reactions and PTSD symptoms. Working with a skilled therapist, they can confront negative thoughts tied to traumatic events and foster more realistic viewpoints through cognitive restructuring, significantly reducing trauma-related anxiety, depression, and other distressing emotions. Practicality is at the core of CBT, focusing on providing first responders with skills and strategies to effectively manage symptoms. They learn deep breathing techniques and grounding exercises to soothe their bodies during distress and are taught to identify and challenge avoidance behaviors to gradually face fears and regain life control.

A key aspect of CBT for first responders is creating a personalized safety plan. This blueprint involves the identification of triggers and the formation of an actionable strategy to address them when they arise. With this roadmap, first responders feel more empowered and can manage their reactions more effectively.

CBT offers a pragmatic, evidence-based solution for first responders dealing with trauma reactions or post-traumatic stress disorder, equipping them with essential skills for their duties and personal lives. First responders experiencing these challenges are not alone, and help is readily available to support both mental health and overall well-being.

Eye Movement Desensitization and Reprocessing (EMDR) Therapy

Eye movement desensitization and reprocessing (EMDR) stands out as one of the most useful interventions for managing post-traumatic reactions and PTSD caused by the demanding roles of first responders. EMDR offers relief, healing, and restoration to those who have encountered distressful events while fulfilling their duties.

Developed in the late 1980s to address PTSD, EMDR has grown into an effective mental health intervention tool. It employs bilateral stimulation, such as eye movements, tapping, or auditory tones, to help clients process traumatized memories safely, aiming to rewire cognitive responses and reduce associated emotional and physiological reactions.

First responders often encounter high-stress situations like life-threatening incidents, witnessing violence, and loss of life that can have profound psychological and emotional ramifications and lead to traumatic reactions and PTSD. EMDR is particularly helpful for these professionals by addressing the emotional and psychological impacts of their challenging work environment.

EMDR therapy is known for its ability to alleviate symptoms quickly and provide lasting relief, offering an advantage over traditional talk therapy, which may take longer to show improvements. This makes EMDR particularly suitable for first responders who need to return to their duties with renewed well-being. Recognized by prominent mental health organizations such as the American Psychiatric Association and the World Health Organization as an evidence-based treatment for trauma, EMDR's credibility as part of the first responder therapy toolkit is well established.

First responders struggling with trauma reactions and PTSD can find hope in EMDR therapy, guided by experienced therapists on healing journeys that facilitate the release of past burdens. Viewing mental health as a priority is a sign of strength and resilience, not weakness. EMDR therapy offers a pathway to liberation from trauma's debilitating effects, promoting lasting well-being.

Exposure Therapy for PTSD

First responders face unique difficulties when it comes to treating post-traumatic stress disorder (PTSD). Their profession exposes them to frequent traumatic events that lead to distressing symptoms that impact both personal and professional aspects. Amid such difficulties stands exposure therapy: an effective approach with great promise for helping first responders navigate PTSD's labyrinthine path of healing.

Exposure therapy, as its name implies, involves confronting memories, thoughts, or situations that serve as triggers for anxiety and distress. At its core lies deliberate exposure of traumatic memories in a safe and controlled environment to gradually gain mastery over emotional responses and take back control over one's life. According to this approach's philosophy, avoidance only serves to reinforce fear and anxiety; by confronting triggers directly it may foster desensitization which ultimately reduces symptoms.

Adopting exposure therapy tailored specifically for first responders' experiences is of utmost importance. For police officers, this may mean revisiting scenes of traumatizing events, engaging in role plays, or viewing videos related to their work; for firefighters, this might involve experiencing fire scenes firsthand; paramedics/EMTs may face challenging calls again while dispatchers and 911 operators find therapeutic relief through simulating emergency calls or exposure to distressing audio recordings.

Exposure therapy presents unique emotional and cognitive challenges; however, it must be remembered that sessions take place within a safe and controlled setting overseen by trained mental health professionals. Therapists serve as compassionate guides throughout each step of exposure therapy for first responders undergoing therapy to ensure their safety and well-being. Over time, individuals engaging in therapy develop new coping skills, gain more control over traumatic memories, and notice a measurable decrease in symptoms associated with posttraumatic stress disorder (PTSD).

First responders cannot underestimate the importance of viewing mental health therapy, specifically exposure therapy, as an act of courage rather than weakness. By facing their trauma related reactions and post-traumatic stress disorder (PTSD), first responders embark on an inspirational journey towards personal healing, ultimately strengthening their capacity to serve and protect communities with enhanced mental well-being.

Group Therapy and Support Networks for First Responders

First responders such as police officers, 911 dispatchers, firefighters, paramedics, and EMTs face specific challenges and traumatic incidents inherent to their roles. These duties often expose them to experiences with profound psychological repercussions, from traumatic reactions and post-traumatic stress disorder (PTSD) to significant impacts on mental health and overall well being. Addressing these complexities effectively requires multifaceted strategies, including group therapy and tailored support networks specifically designed for first responders managing traumatic reactions and PTSD.

Group therapy offers an invaluable intervention, providing a safe space for first responders to share their experiences, emotions, and challenges with peers who understand their unique circumstances. The collective sense of validation, understanding, and support in group therapy reinforces the awareness that they are not alone in their struggles. Sharing narratives among peers can be profoundly empowering.

In the structured environment of group therapy sessions, mental health professionals specializing in trauma therapy guide discussions, offering insights, coping strategies, and practical tools to help first responders cope with trauma reactions and manage PTSD symptoms. These professionals are crucial in fostering healthier coping mechanisms, stress reduction techniques, and overall improvements in mental well-being.

Dedicated support networks, created specifically for first responders experiencing trauma reactions and posttraumatic stress disorder, complement group therapy as an invaluable asset in the recovery journey. Ranging from local to national levels, these networks provide peer support, counseling services, educational materials, and helplines, fostering a strong sense of community and camaraderie among first responders facing similar challenges.

Regular engagement in group therapy or support networks not only offers solace and encouragement to first responders but also practical guidance. These interventions help them better understand traumatic reactions and PTSD, develop effective coping strategies, and build resilience. Beyond meeting immediate mental health needs, these initiatives encourage empowerment and self-care within a supportive community environment.

First responders seeking mental health therapy for trauma-induced reactions and PTSD take a courageous step toward healing and regaining control over their lives. Group therapy and support networks provide invaluable resources and connections to support their ongoing journey of healing and restoration.

Critical Incident Stress Management (CISM) and Critical Incident Response (CIR)

Critical incident stress management (CISM) and critical incident response (CIR) are two forms of mental health therapy specifically tailored to meet the unique challenges that first responders face, serving as integral pillars in providing comprehensive support. These therapeutic concepts offer more than tools for managing the aftermath of crises; they provide dynamic frameworks designed to help individuals navigate the immediate psychological effects and build resilient emotional resilience, aiding their recovery journey.

At the heart of our exploration is critical incident stress management (CISM), which aims to mitigate adverse psychological reactions associated with crisis exposure. Emergency responders, often immersed in high-stakes situations, experience significant emotional tolls. CISM offers a comprehensive, proactive, and supportive system to address these immediate aftermaths.

CISM unfolds as a multidimensional approach, incorporating pre-crisis preparation, acute intervention during events, and post-crisis follow-up. Through debriefing sessions, defusing techniques, and personalized support services, CISM assists first responders in processing their experiences, validating emotions, and building psychological defenses against trauma. This approach not only serves as a reactive measure but also as a preemptive strategy that strengthens mental fortitude before, during, and after crises.

Critical incident response (CIR), on the other hand, provides immediate responses to critical incidents, based on the premise that timely intervention can significantly reduce long-term psychological damage. CIR emphasizes psychological first aid and crisis intervention techniques tailored for first responders, fostering open communication, empathy, and the destigmatization of mental health concerns in environments conducive to its use during critical incidents' aftermaths. Delving into CIR's intricacies reveals its essential role in mental health support services for first responders, offering immediate relief and equipping them to cope with potential challenges in the weeks or months following critical incidents.

Though CISM and CIR are distinct in their approaches, they work together to offer first responders a comprehensive support system, weaving a safety net that extends beyond crisis moments to address both acute and lingering psychological impacts of their demanding profession.

As we proceed through the following chapters, we will examine how CISM and CIR therapies are applied within mental health therapy for first responders. From theoretical foundations to practical applications, our exploration will highlight an approach that fosters resilience and enhances mental well-being, providing guardians of our communities with tools to face not only external challenges but also internal battles following critical incidents.

| 4 |

Chapter 3: Mental Health Therapy for Police Officers

Unique Challenges Faced by Police Officers

Police officers, as protectors of law and order, are exposed to unique challenges that impose considerable strains on their mental wellbeing. This section delves deeper into these complexities, underscoring the critical role of mental health therapy in addressing these issues.

Officers are routinely exposed to violence and traumatic incidents, placing them at the forefront of potentially volatile situations. They witness accidents, crimes, and acts of terrorism, experiences that not only cause emotional trauma but can also leave lasting psychological scars.

Furthermore, the immense responsibility of making split-second, life-or-death decisions adds to the stress, compounded by irregular work hours that disrupt sleep patterns and contribute to mental health issues.

The threat of violent attacks in the line of duty, including threats, ambushes, and direct attacks, creates a constant state of hypervigilance, adversely affecting officers' physical and mental well-being.

Operational challenges and public scrutiny add to the stress, with intense media and public examination of their actions leading to feelings of isolation, mistrust, and burnout. This scrutiny can deter officers from seeking help or openly discussing traumatic events, exacerbating their impact.

Mental health therapy, tailored for police officers, offers hope by providing the tools and support needed to navigate and overcome traumatic reactions and PTSD. Experienced therapists can assist officers in developing coping mechanisms, managing stress, and processing emotions in a non-judgmental environment.

This subchapter aims to raise awareness of the unique challenges faced by police officers and the essential role of mental health therapy in this context. It emphasizes the need for unwavering support and resources to aid those committed to serving and protecting our communities.

Addressing Stigma and Barriers to Mental Health Care within the Police Force

First responders often face stress and must make rapid decisions under high pressure, making mental health a top priority. Effective support for those experiencing trauma reactions or post- traumatic stress disorder (PTSD) is of great importance. In this segment, we delve into the stigmatization and formidable barriers impeding mental health care services in the police force, aiming to illuminate the unique challenges officers face and propose tailored solutions for a more holistic approach.

Police officers, at the forefront of emergency response, are exposed to harrowing incidents that can take a severe psychological toll, leading to emotional distress and PTSD. Unfortunately, stigma surrounding mental health within the police force acts as a barrier to seeking support. An entrenched & "tough guy" culture may perpetuate the idea that seeking mental health help indicates weakness or incompetence, creating a culture of silence that must be dismantled for officers to access the care they deserve.

Addressing this complex issue requires the creation and implementation of mental health therapy programs specifically tailored for police officers. Initiatives should focus on creating a safe, non-judgmental space where officers can express their experiences and emotions without fear of judgment. Normalizing mental health support can help officers overcome stigma and embark on a healing journey.

Acknowledging and overcoming barriers to mental health care, especially access restrictions, is also essential. Many police departments lack the funds and resources for adequate mental health services, making it difficult for officers to access timely and appropriate help. It's imperative that departments allocate sufficient funds and resources to provide accessible mental health services.

Implementing comprehensive training programs to educate police officers and their colleagues about mental health, trauma, and the importance of seeking assistance is vital. Raising awareness and fostering empathy within the force can enable officers to support each other more effectively, promoting an inclusive work environment.

The importance of dismantling stigma and barriers to mental health care within police forces cannot be overstated. By dispelling the stigma surrounding mental illness, providing tailor-made therapy programs, and actively removing access obstacles, police officers can receive the support needed to recover from traumatic reactions and PTSD. Police departments must prioritize their personnel's mental well-being by creating an environment that values mental health support services. Combined efforts will ensure our heroes in blue receive the comprehensive care they deserve.

Specific Therapy Techniques Tailored for Police Officers

Mental health therapy for police officers requires a deep and individualized approach to effectively address traumatic reactions and post-traumatic stress disorder (PTSD). Recognizing their unique experiences and challenges allows therapeutic techniques to be more precise and focused.

Cognitive-behavioral therapy (CBT) is an eddective, tailored psychological intervention for police officers dealing with PTSD symptoms. CBT is particularly relevant in law enforcement, where themes of control, justice, and personal safety are prevalent. It targets negative thoughts and beliefs associated with PTSD symptoms, offering an in-depth approach to managing the psychological aftermath of their experiences.

CBT equips police officers with a transformative way to confront and change their mental frameworks, addressing cognitive distortions specific to law enforcement. Techniques may include cognitive restructuring to challenge maladaptive thoughts, exposure therapy to desensitize individuals to trauma triggers, and mindfulness practices to enhance emotional regulation and situational awareness, building resilience in challenging moments.

By fostering healthier coping mechanisms, CBT reduces the long-term psychological impact of trauma, empowering officers to navigate their complex roles with improved mental well-being and resilience.

Eye movement desensitization and reprocessing (EMDR) is an innovative therapy combining exposure therapy with bilateral stimulation to target trauma recovery. Using eye movements or tapping, EMDR helps police officers process painful memories, re-contextualizing them into more manageable narratives. Bilateral stimulation aids in coping with trauma-related flashbacks and nightmares. EMDR supports officers in processing traumatic experiences, promoting psychological resilience and well-being, showcasing its effectiveness in addressing the unique psychological challenges faced by police officers.

Mindfulness-based stress reduction (MBSR) is a transformative practice rooted in mindfulness meditation, carefully tailored to address the unique challenges police officers face. By incorporating MBSR in law enforcement, officers are encouraged to foster an unwavering presence in every moment, serving as a sanctuary where they can master emotions, cultivate self-compassion, and build resilience.

MBSR offers police officers specific techniques to enhance mental resilience, enabling them to navigate the complex situations inherent in law enforcement. Practices such as focused breathing exercises, body scan meditations, and mindful movement increase awareness, helping officers respond with clarity and composure to stressors.

Beyond immediate stress relief, MBSR's long-term mental health benefits are significant, with studies showing reduced anxiety and depression among officers. Given the constant exposure to stressful environments, resilience-building through MBSR is essential, promoting adaptive coping mechanisms and psychological well-being as foundational elements in officers' mental health support.

Group Therapy and Critical Incident Response complement MBSR as part of a comprehensive mental health strategy for police officers. Group Therapy offers a space for officers to share experiences and explore therapeutic avenues beyond individual sessions, fostering a community of mutual acceptance and support. Structured discussions, role-playing, and guided exercises in a group setting provide diverse coping strategies and resilience-building opportunities.

Critical Incident Response is vital for officers' mental well-being, offering timely support and interventions post-trauma. Tailored debriefing sessions, cognitive-behavioral interventions, and stress management exercises address the unique challenges faced by law enforcement professionals, facilitating quicker recovery from critical incidents.

These therapeutic modalities work synergistically, with Group Therapy providing foundational support and resilience through shared experiences, and Critical Incident Response offering specific interventions during acute stress. Personalization is key; each officer's experiences require a tailored therapeutic approach that considers individual traumas and responses, making mental health therapy an essential ally in reinforcing police officers' resilience in their service to the community.

Effectively addressing the complex challenges affecting police officer mental health requires the development of tailored therapy programs designed specifically for their unique needs. These initiatives must transcend conventional approaches, emphasizing the creation of a secure and nonjudgmental atmosphere. Officers should feel empowered to openly share their experiences and emotions within this space, free from judgment or stigmatization.

By fostering an environment where mental health support is mainstream, these programs aim to dismantle the barriers that prevent officers from embarking on their wellness journey. They promote an active, stigma-free approach to mental health within law enforcement communities, aiding the healing process for those dedicated to public service.

Identifying and resolving impediments to mental health care, especially those related to access constraints, is crucial. A significant part of this issue stems from inadequate resources allocated to mental health services by police departments, which hinders officers' ability to receive timely and adequate care.

To address this challenge, police departments must prioritize and allocate sufficient funding and resources for mental health services. Prioritizing these funds can establish an accessible mental health framework within a department. By considering individual officer mental health needs and systemic limitations, positive steps can be taken toward fostering an environment conducive to law enforcement professionals' mental wellbeing.

Implementation of thorough training programs is of utmost importance to foster mutual understanding among police officers and colleagues concerning mental health, trauma, and the importance of seeking assistance. Comprehensive training initiatives go far beyond simply acknowledging these concepts; they delve deeply into mental health challenges and equip law enforcement professionals with the knowledge and abilities required to manage them effectively. This includes both theoretical and practical strategies designed to teach officers to recognize signs of distress, approach situations with compassion, and organize supportive interventions. The goal of this initiative is not only to disseminate information but also to create a cultural shift within the police force—one that prioritizes mental wellness, promotes open dialogue, and builds an infrastructure of mutual support. By cultivating awareness and empathy within the force, these programs aim to foster an environment characterized by a genuine understanding of one another's struggles, creating an accepting and supportive work atmosphere—ultimately leading to increased efficiency and effectiveness on the field.

The key to improving mental health care within police forces is eradicating stigma and dismantling existing barriers. Our goal should be to create an environment in which law enforcement personnel, known as heroes in blue, can access all the support they deserve without fear or stigmatization. Achieving this requires multifaceted efforts beginning with de- stigmatizing mental health issues through open dialogues that dispel misconceptions surrounding mental illness. Once established, this may bring about cultural shifts that treat seeking help for psychological well-being as a commendable step and encourage all aspects of care to ensure optimal mental wellbeing is seen as commendable rather than something shameful or a needy step.

Implementation of tailored therapy programs is integral to removing stigma. Recognizing the varied mental health needs among police officers, customized therapeutic interventions become critically important. They should address specific challenges and stressors inherent to law enforcement work while offering support for trauma-induced reactions such as post-traumatic stress disorder (PTSD). By tailoring therapeutic approaches specifically to individual police officer needs, officers can receive effective care that responds directly to their experiences.

Dismantling barriers to care is crucial, necessitating proactive efforts to identify and eliminate any impediments that might deter officers from seeking or receiving the support they need. These could be logistical difficulties, bureaucratic roadblocks, or cultural resistance within police departments—a comprehensive effort is essential to ensure unfettered access to mental health resources.

Police departments have the responsibility to prioritize mental well-being by fostering an organizational culture that values mental health support services. Creating an environment that emphasizes psychological well-being among officers can improve the likelihood of them seeking assistance when necessary. Such proactive measures not only bolster mental health within police forces but also guarantee that our law enforcement heroes receive the holistic and comprehensive care they deserve. Through these efforts, law enforcement agencies can make a significant contribution to enhancing resilience and well-being among those who selflessly serve our communities.

| 5 |

Chapter 4: Mental Health Therapy for Firefighters

Understanding the Psychological Impact of Firefighting

Firefighting, while widely recognized for its noble virtues, also presents immense challenges that extend beyond the physical risks of combating fires. The psychological toll often falls into the background. This exploration seeks to dissect the specific psychological hurdles inherent to firefighting and highlight the vital role of mental health therapy in treating any potential post- traumatic stress disorder (PTSD) experienced by these valiant first responders.

Firefighters' daily lives are filled with stressful encounters, from witnessing fatalities and severe injuries to confronting the willful destruction of property. Such experiences can have an enormous psychological impact, often leading to symptoms of post-traumatic stress disorder (PTSD) like intrusive thoughts, nightmares, hypervigilance, and avoidance behaviors. Concurrent struggles with depression, anxiety, and substance abuse may also manifest, requiring nuanced understanding and targeted intervention strategies.

Engaging in mental health therapy is essential for firefighters to address the psychological fallout of their experiences. Therapy provides a confidential space to explore emotions, build coping strategies, and learn stress and anxiety management techniques. It also addresses the unique challenges within the firefighting profession, such as peer pressure to remain strong and stigma around mental illness.

Therapy offers firefighters grappling with trauma-induced reactions and post-traumatic stress disorder (PTSD) an essential lifeline. It not only diminishes distressing symptoms but also substantially improves overall quality of life, acting as an anchor against further psychological degradation. Specialized therapists use tailored treatment modalities like cognitive-behavioral therapy (CBT), eye movement desensitization and reprocessing (EMDR), or group therapy to meet individual needs.

Peer support groups and critical incident stress management (CISM) programs highlight the power of teamwork alongside individual therapy. Sharing stories in these support networks creates camaraderie and mutual understanding among firefighters, breaking down isolation and forging bonds that promote a supportive culture within the profession.

The psychological impacts of firefighting are complex and must be carefully addressed. Given the increased risk of trauma reactions and post-traumatic stress disorder inherent to their profession, firefighters must proactively engage in mental health therapy to maintain their strength, resilience, and compassion. By acknowledging and treating the psychological wounds of their profession, firefighters enhance their dedication and effectiveness in their duties.

Overcoming the Stigma of Mental Health in the Fire Service

Mental health in first responders often gets overlooked or burdened by social stigmas. This section explores the unique challenges firefighters face when seeking mental health therapy, sheds light on pervasive stigmatization, and explores strategies for dismantling these barriers. We aim to understand all obstacles preventing firefighters from prioritizing their mental well-being and to foster in-depth knowledge of their complex environment.

It's important to recognize the unique challenges of the firefighting profession, such as frequent exposure to traumatic incidents and post-traumatic stress disorder (PTSD). By acknowledging the psychological toll on firefighters and studying trauma reactions, this subchapter seeks to dismantle stigma by normalizing mental health discourse and removing inhibitions to therapeutic intervention.

This exploration aims to create a plan for transformative change by unraveling stigma and dismantling preconceived notions, fostering an environment where seeking mental health therapy is not only recommended and welcomed but also viewed as an essential component of firefighter well-being.

Addressing mental health in the fire service involves exploring complex interactions among social perceptions, organizational dynamics, and individual resilience. We seek to understand current obstacles and chart a path toward a future where mental health is prioritized without stigma or discrimination.

Understanding the Stigma:

As part of exploring the complexity and nuance surrounding mental health stigma within the fire service, it becomes critical to examine its interplay with celebrated virtues such as bravery, resilience, and unwavering strength, against acknowledging and addressing mental health challenges. Firefighting communities often pride themselves on embodying such traits; yet, when it comes to vulnerability or reaching out for assistance during psychological distress, they encounter barriers that prevent acceptance or intervention.

Mental health stigma within the fire service stems from multiple issues, most notably anxiety about appearing weak or inadequate for firefighting duties. Society typically values strength over vulnerability, often viewing emotional struggles as incongruent with the archetype of a fearless firefighter. Fear of perceived weakness acts as an immense deterrent against openly acknowledging mental health challenges or seeking professional assistance.

The ripples of this pervasive stigma extend far beyond an individual firefighter and permeate every layer of firefighting culture. A reluctance to address mental health concerns creates an atmosphere where seeking assistance becomes discouraged, inadvertently perpetuating an endless cycle of silence and denial that leads to more silence and denial from colleagues, creating a collective ethos that prioritizes upholding an appearance of invulnerability over the well-being of its members.

Unraveling and dismantling this stigma requires an in-depth knowledge of the unique psychological pressures inherent to firefighting, along with an acceptance that seeking help is not indicative of weakness but proactive steps toward maintaining mental well-being for those devoted to protecting others' safety. Initiatives designed to encourage open dialogue, reduce stereotypes, and provide accessible mental health resources are critical interventions toward creating a culture that prioritizes the psychological welfare of firefighters, thus strengthening resilience across the firefighting community.

Breaking the Silence:

Breaking the silence around mental health within the fire service requires an all-inclusive strategy that delves into the community fabric. It's essential to go beyond merely acknowledging mental health challenges and to build an atmosphere of understanding, empathy, and proactive support for firefighters.

Creating a safe and supportive environment demands tangible actions that dismantle barriers to open conversations. Fire departments should initiate efforts that recognize mental health issues and destigmatize seeking help. This may include formal policies and fostering an environment where firefighters can share their experiences without fear of judgment or reprisal.

Encouraging open dialogue is important, but it's just one aspect of a comprehensive approach. Education and awareness are equally important. Firefighters need access to information that clarifies mental health challenges and dispels myths about seeking help. Incorporating workshops, training, and awareness campaigns into fire service culture is vital for promoting a holistic view of mental well-being.

The power of personal narratives in changing perceptions should not be underestimated. Stories of overcoming mental health challenges can profoundly impact how help-seeking is viewed within the fire service. Seeing peers share their experiences and positive outcomes can shift the perception of seeking help from one of weakness to one of strength and courage.

To truly break the silence around mental health in the fire service, a paradigm shift is needed. This shift must encompass policies, programs, and a change in collective attitudes. By fostering an environment that values vulnerability and mental wellness, and by celebrating the act of seeking help, fire services can cultivate a more compassionate and supportive atmosphere for all members.

Training and Education:

Comprehensive mental health training should be a core part of every firefighter's career. Departments need to mandate in-depth mental health education programs that not only help in recognizing symptoms of trauma reactions or post-traumatic stress disorder (PTSD) but also highlight early intervention strategies and encourage a proactive approach within the firefighting community.

Training should delve deeper than basic awareness, equipping firefighters with a deep understanding of the psychological challenges unique to their roles. This includes stress management techniques and coping mechanisms tailored to firefighting, as well as a broad education on mental health that enables firefighters to identify signs of distress in themselves and others, and understand mental wellness more broadly.

Cultivating a culture where mental health issues are normalized is essential. Departments should promote a shared responsibility for mental health and encourage open discussions about challenges, helping to dismantle barriers to seeking help. Equipping firefighters with the knowledge and tools to address their mental health needs will support both their psychological well-being and professional performance.

For mental health education in the fire service to be effective, it must transcend traditional approaches and include comprehensive understanding, proactive strategies, and a cultural shift towards normalizing help-seeking. Such a comprehensive approach is crucial for empowering firefighters to prioritize and maintain their mental health throughout their careers.

Providing Confidential and Accessible Resources:

To establish an effective support system for firefighters' mental well-being, fire departments must prioritize creating reliable mechanisms that provide secure and easily accessible mental health resources. This may involve forming strategic partnerships with mental health specialists who have expertise in first responder challenges; proactive engagement with these specialists can help departments create an environment that acknowledges and addresses the psychological aspects of firefighting.

Fire departments aiming to maximize mental health support effectiveness should offer more than generic counseling services, focusing instead on custom interventions tailored to firefighters' unique experiences. Therapy that addresses the specific stressors, traumas, and demands of their duty can significantly benefit firefighters, offering a space that recognizes and validates their experiences and concerns.

Confidentiality is a key component of encouraging firefighters to seek help. Departments should ensure the privacy of therapy sessions, reassuring firefighters that discussions with mental health professionals remain confidential. This assurance can help alleviate concerns about judgment or repercussions, fostering a trusting environment where firefighters can openly discuss mental health challenges.

Accessibility to mental health resources is essential. Departments should streamline access to these services, integrating support into overall health and wellness programs, creating straightforward channels for assistance, and consistently informing personnel about available resources.

Fire departments' commitment to their personnel's mental health involves a comprehensive approach that includes strategic partnerships, tailored interventions, confidentiality, and improved access. Such consistent measures can cultivate a resilient, supportive environment that prioritizes firefighters' psychological well-being, thereby strengthening the firefighting community.

Supportive Peer Networks:

Establishing strong and supportive peer networks within the fire service is paramount for dismantling mental health stigma among firefighters. Rather than merely recognizing the importance of such networks, integrating them into the organizational culture is essential. This integration allows firefighters to form deep, meaningful relationships that facilitate open discussions about mental health without fear of judgment or reprisal.

Peer-led support groups and structured buddy systems are effective strategies for enhancing this support, moving beyond superficial interactions to provide intentional, ongoing assistance. Groups led by peers who have faced similar challenges offer unique benefits, as these leaders can share personal experiences that promote empathy and understanding, helping to break down barriers and underscore that mental health issues are a professional reality.

Buddy systems, in particular, provide a tangible form of mutual support, pairing firefighters in ways that extend beyond their professional responsibilities to help each other through the complexities of mental health. This structured approach ensures a reliable support system, fostering emotional resilience and strengthening community bonds.

Open and honest conversations about mental health within these networks are vital for reducing stigma. Normalizing such discussions raises awareness and creates an environment where seeking help is viewed as a sign of strength. Emphasizing that mental health support is a critical aspect of peer networks highlights the importance of reaching out for personal and professional well-being.

Building supportive peer networks in the fire service demands active commitment, not just acknowledgment. By embedding these supportive connections into the very fabric of firefighting culture, we can diminish the stigma around mental health and lay a resilient, supportive foundation for those dedicated to our protection and safety.

Conclusion:

Reducing mental health stigma within the fire service requires a holistic and collaborative effort among fire departments, mental health providers, and individual firefighters. To achieve substantial transformation, a multidimensional cultural shift is essential, centered on unwavering support, continuing education, and open dialogue. This shift aims to firmly establish mental health therapy as a core component of firefighters' holistic well-being. By dismantling barriers to discussions on mental health, therapeutic interventions can become an integral part of firefighter wellness. Collectively, we pursue a path toward healing our heroes by offering them the comprehensive mental health support they richly deserve. It necessitates a systematic reevaluation and restructuring of existing norms to create an environment that not only acknowledges but actively addresses the psychological challenges inherent to the profession. Through our joint efforts, seeking mental health assistance should be viewed not as a sign of weakness but as an essential and courageous step toward maintaining the mental resilience required for the essential duties of firefighters.

Therapeutic Strategies for Firefighters Battling Traumatic Reactions and PTSD

Introduction:

Firefighters, known for their outstanding commitment and altruistic service in protecting communities, face numerous hardships as part of their noble profession. Their courageous efforts in dangerous environments come with significant psychological repercussions that may prove lifelong. This includes but is not limited to elevated stress levels, widespread anxiety, and the gradual development of post-traumatic stress disorder (PTSD). Recognizing their experiences are unique, this subchapter explores the complex dynamics that contribute to psychological fatigue in firefighters. Therefore, this study seeks to provide a comprehensive exploration of therapeutic strategies specially crafted to address their unique challenges, with the aim of not simply mitigating but actively aiding in the resolution of trauma reactions and effective management of PTSD for this resilient but vulnerable demographic.

Understanding Traumatic Reactions:

Firefighters face an array of complex and demanding environments while carrying out their duties, from distressing scenes and personal threats to the bereavement of colleagues. Such traumatizing experiences may have long-lasting repercussions for their psychological well-being, often manifesting through nightmares, flashbacks, or increased states of arousal as a response to these incidents.

Understanding traumatic reactions within the fire service requires an in-depth exploration of all its stressors, from witnessing human suffering and personal safety concerns to loss and potential personal tragedies. These build over time, becoming cumulative effects that impact every incident and each individual firefighter may struggle with not only acute stressors but also their cumulative experiences over time.

Recognizing trauma's signs is crucial in supporting firefighters' mental health. This involves understanding psychological and physiological responses; beyond obvious signs like nightmares and flashbacks, there may also be more subtle indications such as changes in mood, sleep patterns, or interpersonal relationships that point toward its devastating effects.

Firefighters need access to appropriate mental health therapy as part of their overall well- being. Support should not only address visible symptoms but also the psychological processes at play. Furthermore, the stigma associated with seeking assistance must be dismantled to create an environment where firefighters feel empowered to prioritize their mental well-being.

An effective understanding of traumatic reactions in the fire service requires looking into their unique challenges, acknowledging cumulative experiences, and noting any overt or subtle signs of distress while advocating for accessible mental health support within their community.

Cognitive-Behavioral Therapy (CBT):

Cognitive-behavioral therapy (CBT) stands out as an incredibly potent and flexible therapeutic modality when applied to the special challenges faced by firefighters coping with trauma reactions and post-traumatic stress disorder (PTSD). CBT delves into cognitive processes, seeking out and dissecting negative thoughts and beliefs linked to intense incidents in the line of duty that have become entrenched as part of one's subconscious reactions to trauma.

CBT is an effective intervention within the fire service context, where exposure to trauma is an inherent occupational hazard. It guides firefighters on an inward journey of self-discovery to unearth and dissect cognitive distortions that contribute to emotional distress, while at the same time unmasking an interconnected web of thoughts that perpetuate psychological suffering.

For firefighters, CBT goes beyond mere identification to incorporate targeted strategies that effectively challenge and reframe maladaptive cognitive patterns. Firefighters are equipped with cognitive tools and techniques designed to counter negative thought processes, creating cognitive resilience against trauma experiences. Sessions combine evidence-based cognitive interventions with behavioral techniques in an integrative fashion for optimal therapy outcomes that address both physical and emotional aspects of trauma.

CBT in the fire service emphasizes cognitive restructuring and skill acquisition. Firefighters receive training in coping mechanisms and relaxation techniques tailored to their occupational requirements, providing them with indispensable resources to handle the intense pressures inherent to their profession. From mindfulness practices to stress inoculation training, CBT offers a holistic toolkit for improving emotional regulation and resilience.

CBT helps develop a more balanced outlook toward traumatic experiences by offering alternative cognitive interpretations and reframing distressing events as meaning-laden events, enabling firefighters to develop a resilient mindset that promotes post-traumatic growth. The therapeutic alliance established between the firefighter and practitioner serves as the conduit for this transformative process, fostering trust and open communication, which are key to successfully navigating the therapeutic journey.

Cognitive-behavioral therapy represents not just a treatment modality but a profound paradigm shift for firefighters' psychological well-being. By engaging with the intricacies of cognition and behavior, CBT enables firefighters to manage trauma-related stressors more effectively and emerge with a renewed sense of purpose in the challenging landscape of fire service work.

Eye Movement Desensitization and Reprocessing (EMDR):

Eye movement desensitization and reprocessing (EMDR) stands out as a carefully tailored therapeutic approach designed specifically to address the psychological difficulties experienced by firefighters after traumatizing incidents. At its core, EMDR investigates traumatic memories to understand their impact on mental well-being; unlike conventional therapeutic approaches, this one operates on the principle that distressful memories can be effectively processed through specific bilateral stimulation techniques.

EMDR therapy for fire service personnel extends beyond mere acknowledgment of past traumas. It involves a strategic examination of memories within a safe environment, utilizing eye movements to alleviate the emotional charges tied to distressful memories. Through guided and systematic approaches, firefighters engage in the EMDR process, reducing the intensity of these memories and actively shaping their emotional responses.

EMDR aims not just at symptom reduction but at fostering emotional control and resilience among firefighters. The therapy involves delving into layers of trauma, aiding individuals in confronting and reprocessing distressing aspects of their experiences within a secure therapeutic setting, led by an EMDR-trained therapist.

EMDR for the fire service offers a holistic and comprehensive approach to trauma recovery, recognizing and adapting its therapeutic interventions to meet their specific challenges. By integrating bilateral stimulation and guided eye movements, EMDR not only seeks to mitigate immediate distress from traumatic memories but also aims to establish long-term emotional balance and empowerment for its participants.

Group Therapy:

Group therapy within the context of fire service provides an invaluable and specialized therapeutic approach that addresses the specific challenges firefighters face after experiencing trauma. It offers an invaluable chance for individuals within this profession to form deep connections with peers who share similar experiences, creating an atmosphere of empathy and solidarity. This setting opens dialogue about trauma experiences, providing a space where catharsis and validation may occur simultaneously.

For firefighters, group therapy extends beyond mere storytelling to offer multifaceted emotional support. Participants can express their struggles and actively participate in the healing process of fellow firefighters. This reciprocal dynamic enhances collective resilience as individuals collaborate to manage post-traumatic stress and its aftermath, discovering different approaches to handle its profound psychological consequences.

Group therapy effectively counters the overwhelming sense of isolation that often accompanies traumatic incidents in fire service. By bringing together individuals with similar professional backgrounds, it helps dispel the feeling that others cannot fully understand the unique rigors and challenges of firefighting. The collective wisdom within groups strengthens and helps alleviate the emotional burden for firefighters.

In the fire service, group therapy transcends conventional therapeutic intervention, creating an integrative and comprehensive approach to healing. Leveraging shared experiences, mutual support, and the exchange of coping strategies as foundational elements, it offers a holistic path to recovery for firefighters.

Mindfulness and Meditation:

Mindfulness and meditation provide an invaluable therapeutic remedy for firefighters coping with trauma reactions and PTSD. These contemplative techniques offer a nuanced approach to cognitive and emotional well-being, enhancing present-moment awareness and allowing firefighters to fully engage with life as it unfolds.

Mindfulness has become an invaluable tool in the fire service, aiding firefighters in navigating the emotional aftermath of distressing experiences. By focusing on the present and fostering a nonjudgmental awareness of thoughts and emotions, mindfulness facilitates a transformative therapeutic journey, fostering profound self-awareness and breaking through barriers of self- criticism.

Beyond fostering internal awareness, mindfulness aids firefighters in mastering emotional regulation, moving beyond traditional coping mechanisms. Regular mindfulness practice enhances the ability to respond calmly and objectively to stressful situations, combining focused attention with non-reactive awareness to mitigate the negative impacts of stress and trauma.

Mindfulness and meditation in the fire service offer more than stress management; they initiate an introspective journey that delves into the dynamics between mind and emotion. Embracing these practices, firefighters embark on a transformative path toward resilience, self- mastery, and an unwavering presence amidst the unpredictable challenges of their profession.

Peer Support Programs:

Peer support programs, critical incident stress management (CISM), and critical incident response (CIR) are integral parts of a holistic therapeutic approach tailored to meet the unique challenges encountered by firefighting communities. Peer support programs play an essential role that surpasses mere camaraderie, serving as early intervention programs that contribute towards psychological well-being for firefighters from the moment that an incident occurs, and long afterward as well. They foster open dialogue and create an environment that emphasize vulnerability through shared experiences, encouraging a culture that values open communication.

The importance of critical incident stress management (CISM) in firefighting, a profession fraught with occupational hazards, cannot be understated. This approach addresses the aftermath of critical incidents, offering structured interventions to mitigate psychological effects on firefighters, with pre-incident training, crisis interventions, and post-incident follow-ups forming its comprehensive nature.

Critical incident response (CIR) complements this therapeutic framework by providing a systematic approach for managing the effects of critical incidents within fire service agencies. CIR offers proactive strategies for preparation and response, thereby enhancing resilience at both individual and organizational levels.

Peer support programs, CISM, and CIR create a vital environment to protect the mental health and well-being of firefighters. By acknowledging the unique challenges of firefighting careers and creating a support system that extends beyond basic camaraderie—through open dialogue, sharing practical advice, providing safe spaces for vulnerability, and encouraging open communication—these frameworks aim to build resilience, thus safeguarding sustained psychological well-being despite the demanding and potentially traumatizing duties.

Conclusion

Firefighters face unique challenges in their line of duty, often exposed to traumatic incidents that can trigger severe emotional repercussions including post-traumatic stress disorder (PTSD). Addressing their mental health needs requires a tailored approach, with strategies that go beyond conventional therapy interventions.

Individual mental health therapy offers firefighters a valuable means to process their experiences in a safe and confidential space, allowing them to explore emotions, process trauma, and develop coping mechanisms. Therapists specializing in trauma can help firefighters manage the unique stressors of their profession.

Group support plays a crucial role in building community among firefighters. Group therapy sessions tailored for firefighters allow them to openly discuss challenges, share coping strategies, and draw strength from shared experiences. This approach reduces the isolation associated with trauma and fosters a healing environment.

Mindfulness practices are an integral component of firefighters' mental health care. By practicing meditation and stress reduction exercises, firefighters can improve emotional regulation and resilience. Mindfulness also helps develop a greater awareness of thoughts and emotions, enabling more adaptive responses to stress and reducing trauma's impact on psychological well-being.

Additionally, an inclusive approach to mental health care involves training fire service personnel and leadership to recognize early signs of distress and to create a culture that normalizes seeking help. This atmosphere encourages individuals to prioritize their mental well being, preventing psychological challenges from worsening.

At its core, a multifaceted therapeutic approach that includes individual therapy, group support, mindfulness practices, and a proactive organizational culture is necessary to meet the mental health needs of firefighters. Adopting these strategies can help fire services reduce the adverse effects of trauma and equip members to navigate its complexities while maintaining robust mental health and well-being.

Chapter 5: Mental Health Therapy for Paramedics and EMTs

The Emotional Toll of Emergency Medical Response

As emergency medical response draws attention to itself through stories of heroism from first responders, it becomes vitally important to observe and evaluate their mental health in tandem. Beyond stories of bravery, there's another layer to their profession—an emotional toll from its unyielding demands.

As heroes who rush into life-threatening situations, they witness the stark realities of life and death. Scenes etched onto their consciousness remain forever: anguished cries, mournful loss of life, and exposure to traumatizing events. These experiences go far beyond superficial stories of bravery, leading to mental health challenges as diverse as the emergencies faced.

Posttraumatic stress disorder (PTSD), anxiety, depression, and burnout transcend clinical terminology. They represent daily struggles against distressing experiences that threaten mental well-being, revealing the true cost of emergency medical response in these emotional crucibles.

Comparative analyses between paramedics, emergency medical technicians (EMTs), and other first responders like police officers and firefighters reveal distinct emotional landscapes. Police officers grapple with the continual exposure to violence and crime, affecting their sense of safety and trust. Firefighters, on the other hand, confront the trauma of witnessing property destruction and loss of life. While firefighters face such trauma firsthand, the experiences of paramedics and EMTs are often marked by survivor's guilt and feelings of helplessness, adding complexity to their emotional journey.

This exploration of their emotional terrain highlights that their challenges go beyond external threats to mental resilience. By acknowledging and addressing these issues, they show not vulnerability, but a recognition of humanity as an integral part of heroic action - it's about understanding that to safeguard others, one must first protect oneself.

Paramedics and EMTs are immersed in high-stakes medical emergencies, constantly navigating life-or-death decisions. Their daily reality involves making critical choices for those in crisis, while the exposure to such high-stakes situations fosters a profound sense of responsibility, even amidst factors beyond their control.

Paramedics and EMTs face unique mental health challenges not just from witnessing traumatic events, but also from the far-reaching effects of such experiences. Compassion fatigue, characterized by a gradual loss of empathy and emotional strength, is an inherent risk in professions demanding immediate aid. Emotional exhaustion from witnessing human suffering and making critical decisions contributes to a complex set of difficulties within emergency medical fields.

Those not directly involved in medical response, such as dispatchers and 911 operators, also experience emotional strain. They face vicarious trauma from distressing calls and the pressure to provide timely assistance, leading to emotional fatigue and highlighting the widespread emotional toll across emergency response systems.

Understanding the profound effects of these experiences is key to addressing mental health challenges in paramedics and EMTs. The emotional impact of managing trauma incidents and high-stakes scenarios underscores the need for mental health therapy tailored to these frontline heroes.

Investigating therapeutic intervention reveals a comprehensive framework tailored to the psychological needs of first responders with trauma reactions and PTSD. This therapy isn't just an invaluable lifeline; it's an indispensable resource providing structure and support for navigating the complex emotional landscape inherent in emergency medical response work.

Expertly administered therapeutic sessions offer a haven for paramedics and EMTs. These sessions provide a space to process and understand the harrowing experiences encountered in their duties, facilitating stress management, the development of resilient coping mechanisms, the freedom to express emotions without judgment, and genuine healing.

Therapy is more than just an emotional outlet; it's a dynamic tool equipping first responders with skills beyond coping, enhancing overall resilience. It also offers a chance to develop communication strategies, understand oneself better, and strengthen relationships with loved ones, who are often cornerstones of their support network.

Rejecting the notion that seeking help is a sign of weakness is vital; rather, it demonstrates the strength, resilience, and dedication of paramedics and EMTs. Prioritizing mental health therapy is not just a personal obligation; it's a monumental step towards healing, enabling these professionals to continue serving and protecting the community effectively, fostering healthier approaches to their demanding work environment.

Promoting Mental Health Awareness and Support Systems in EMS

Emergency medical services (EMS) professionals, encompassing police officers, firefighters, paramedics, EMTs, and 911 dispatchers, face challenging events daily as part of their duties. These unsung heroes confront situations that can severely impact their psychological well- being. Recognizing the importance of mental health intervention for those enduring trauma reactions or post-traumatic stress disorder (PTSD) is critical in an EMS community culture that aims to raise mental health awareness.

It's evident from this investigation that the challenges EMS professionals face go beyond physical demands, encompassing mental resilience and psychological stressors. Quick decision- making under immense pressure and handling unexpected emergencies contribute to unique forms of anxiety. The societal expectation for first responders to maintain a constant facade of strength adds to their mental health strain, underscoring the need for a mental wellbeing- supportive environment for EMS personnel.

Central to this paradigm shift is the development and promotion of mental health awareness initiatives specifically tailored for the EMS community. Educating stakeholders within the EMS system and the broader public about the unique challenges first responders face is crucial. This includes disseminating information on psychological impacts related to their duties and combating misconceptions about mental health in this context. Additionally, these initiatives should aim to eliminate the stigma around seeking support, fostering an atmosphere where vulnerability is recognized as a sign of strength.

Implementing strong support systems is as vital as awareness efforts, requiring comprehensive mental health programs within EMS organizations. This should encompass regular mental health check-ins, access to confidential counseling, and proactive stress-reduction measures. Cultivating a culture of peer support and camaraderie can also mitigate the isolating effects of trauma, while creating safe spaces for open dialogue can bolster resilience and psychological well-being among EMS professionals.

Advocating for mental health in emergency response services goes beyond acknowledgment; it demands an integrated, proactive approach. By fostering an environment of awareness, understanding, and strong support within their community, EMS organizations can enhance mental resilience among members and drive a change in how mental health is perceived and prioritized in this challenging field.

Understanding the link between mental and physical well-being is important in EMS. Addressing the pervasive stigma around discussing mental health issues is key for meaningful change, necessitating effective strategies to dismantle this barrier.

Fostering an environment of openness and understanding is essential for increasing mental health awareness among EMS professionals. This involves not just acknowledging mental health issues but also actively creating a culture where seeking help is encouraged and supported. Education and training programs are pivotal in this shift. They need to be designed with the unique challenges faced by EMS personnel in mind, addressing the specific stressors they encounter daily.

These programs serve two main purposes for emergency response professionals. Firstly, they help EMS community members recognize signs and symptoms of mental health conditions in themselves and others. Secondly, they promote proactive approaches to mental well-being, encouraging preventive measures and resilience against the stressors of emergency response work.

A multifaceted approach is necessary for effective mental health awareness and support in EMS. This includes dispelling the stigma around mental illness and providing targeted educational interventions. These initiatives equip professionals with the insights and skills needed for mental well-being. Such efforts can lead to a first responder community that values mental well-being as much as physical well-being.

Enhancing mental health awareness and support systems in EMS requires an integrated strategy, using multiple tactics for members' well-being. Implementing robust peer support programs, tailored to the specific challenges of EMS professionals, is crucial. These programs enable first responders to leverage shared experiences to build supportive bonds, helping manage the emotional traumas inherent in their work.

Establishing safe spaces within the EMS community is vital. These areas act as havens for open and honest discussions about mental health, free from judgment by colleagues or superiors. They create a setting of vulnerability where sharing experiences and challenges is encouraged. This not only builds individual resilience but also cultivates a collective culture of support and understanding among peers.

Integrating peer support programs and safe spaces is an effective strategy for enhancing mental health in EMS, fostering an environment where mental well-being is a priority. By working together, the EMS community can break down the stigma around mental illness and provide the necessary resources to handle the emotional challenges and taxing nature of the profession.

Promoting mental health awareness and strengthening support systems in EMS requires a multifaceted approach. It's clear that providing access to specialized mental health therapy services is critical. These services, specifically tailored to first responders dealing with trauma reactions and PTSD, are pivotal.

Mental health therapy for EMS personnel is much more than psychological support; it's an invaluable asset. It provides a secure, confidential space where they can process their experiences without the pressure of immediate symptom relief. Therapy also serves as a forum for first responders to thoughtfully process encounters, manage stress and anxiety, and develop coping mechanisms specifically suited to their profession. This acts as a sanctuary for introspection and growth, building resilience against the challenges faced in daily work life.

The effectiveness of mental health therapy hinges on its accessibility, affordability, and suitability for EMS personnel. It's essential for stakeholders to ensure that therapy services are not just available, but also well-integrated into EMS support systems. This involves initiatives to bridge the gap between mental health resources and the daily realities of first responders, breaking down barriers that might prevent them from seeking help.

Championing mental health awareness within EMS necessitates a thorough evaluation of existing support structures. Special focus should be given to creating an environment that acknowledges and addresses the significant psychological impact on these professionals, while also offering tailored therapeutic interventions to meet their unique challenges.

Integrating mental health considerations into emergency medical service (EMS) organizations is crucial for creating a resilient and supportive working environment. More than just recognizing mental health awareness and support systems, it involves fully incorporating them into the organization's culture and operations. Regular mental health check-ins should be established, allowing individuals to openly discuss their emotional well-being without fear of stigma or judgment. Additionally, proactive measures like resilience training are essential, equipping EMS personnel with tools to handle the unique stressors of their profession.

Promoting mental health needs to be a continuous commitment woven into daily operations, not just periodic interventions. This includes fostering a work environment that supports a healthy work-life balance and prioritizes self-care practices. Such an approach develops an organizational culture that acknowledges and actively addresses the psychological challenges faced by EMS professionals.

A key aspect of this cultural transformation is eliminating stigma associated with seeking mental health support. Creating an environment where mental well-being is encouraged helps break down barriers preventing individuals from seeking help. A culture that prioritizes mental health enhances overall well-being, serving as a preventive measure against burnout and other mental health adversities in high-pressure environments like EMS.

Advocating for mental health awareness and robust support systems within the EMS community is critical. Understanding its effects is paramount; creating comprehensive support infrastructures involves acknowledging and proactively establishing multifaceted assistance networks. This is especially important for first responders dealing with trauma-induced PTSD. Ensuring easy access to specialized therapeutic interventions is necessary for optimizing the well-being of those suffering from these conditions.

Organizational culture change within EMS is also essential. By integrating mental health considerations into their core practices, EMS organizations adopt a holistic approach to mental well-being. This includes destigmatization, open discussion, and prioritizing mental health alongside physical well-being. Collaborative efforts in this direction can help heal the emotional and psychological wounds of these unsung heroes, reinforcing resilience and maintaining a steadfast commitment to community safety.

Effective Therapy Approaches for Paramedics and EMTs

Introduction

First responders such as paramedics and emergency medical technicians (EMTs) often encounter situations that have an overwhelming effect on their psychological well-being. Their work in emergency settings exposes them to trauma, leaving a lasting effect on their mental health. This subchapter delves into therapeutic interventions tailored for this intrepid group. Our exploration extends beyond a superficial examination, revealing layered approaches aimed at fostering psychological recovery and fortitude.

For paramedics and EMTs dealing with the complexities of trauma, understanding its full spectrum of challenges is imperative. This chapter aims to provide evidence-based treatments and methodologies, acting as a guide towards healing and resilience. Our objective is not merely to scratch the surface; we seek to deepen our comprehension of the therapeutic landscape, customizing it for the unique needs of the first responder community. By exploring effective therapy approaches, our goal is to establish a strong foundation for the psychological well-being of paramedics and EMTs, empowering them to effectively confront and overcome the traumas inherent in their honorable profession.

Trauma-Focused Cognitive Behavioral Therapy (TF-CBT):

Trauma-focused cognitive behavioral therapy (TF-CBT) offers a sophisticated, evidence based therapeutic framework, specifically addressing the unique needs of paramedics and emergency medical technicians (EMTs) coping with posttraumatic experiences. Central to TF-CBT is the integration of cognitive and behavioral interventions for comprehensive trauma recovery. This process also tackles cognitive distortions, emotional changes, or maladaptive behaviors stemming from traumatic events.

Paramedics and EMTs, frequently encountering high-stakes and emotionally charged situations, often find TF-CBT invaluable in managing post-traumatic stress. The therapy involves examining negative thoughts triggered by trauma, unraveling associated emotional responses, and understanding behavioral patterns that have emerged as adaptive responses to these challenges.

TF-CBT also considers the specific challenges paramedics and EMTs face in their roles. It takes into account factors pertinent to emergency response scenarios and focuses on developing coping skills specifically for such situations. By analyzing the interplay of thoughts, emotions, and behaviors, TF-CBT enables first responders to better understand their reactions and regain control over their psychological responses.

TF-CBT extends beyond symptom reduction, providing paramedics and EMTs with a comprehensive psychological toolkit for use beyond clinical settings. This approach not only eases immediate PTSD symptoms but also promotes lasting psychological resilience. It engages individuals in a transformative process, helping them manage the aftermath of trauma and thrive in their demanding roles.

As an innovative and holistic approach, TF-CBT acknowledges the complex interaction between cognitive processes, emotions, and behaviors in trauma. Tailored to the specific challenges of first responders, it aims not just to alleviate symptoms but to foster enduring resilience, equipping them with the psychological strength needed for their challenging roles.

Eye Movement Desensitization and Reprocessing (EMDR):

Eye Movement Desensitization and Reprocessing (EMDR) is an innovative therapeutic approach tailored for paramedics and Emergency Medical Technicians (EMTs) to address their unique psychological challenges. EMDR uses bilateral stimulation techniques, typically eye movements, in a safe therapeutic setting to reprocess traumatic memories. This method enables paramedics and EMTs to access and explore their distressing experiences under careful supervision.

In this controlled therapeutic environment, EMDR encourages a deep exploration and restructuring of the emotional and cognitive elements associated with traumatic experiences. This approach allows paramedics and EMTs to work through their distressing experiences in an intimate setting, focusing on restructuring related emotional and cognitive elements.

Paramedics and EMTs, who often encounter intense or traumatic incidents in their professional lives, can find EMDR to be a particularly effective intervention tailored to their needs. This therapy's structured approach allows them to gradually desensitize distressing memories through controlled eye movements, reducing the emotional intensity attached to these memories. Cognitive processing techniques like eye tracking are then used to reframe these memories into more adaptive narratives with reduced emotional attachment.

EMDR therapy provides paramedics and EMTs with a safe space to address and process their traumatic experiences. A trained EMDR therapist facilitates a protective environment where individuals can explore their experiences fully, without the fear of being overwhelmed by emotions. The guided eye movements in EMDR not only assist in reprocessing memories but also help individuals draw connections between past distressing events and their current emotional state.

The comprehensive approach of EMDR extends beyond mere symptom alleviation. It aims to foster lasting healing and resilience among paramedics and EMTs. By systematically reprocessing traumatic memories, EMDR helps to unravel the complex web of emotions, thoughts, and sensations linked to distressing events, enabling individuals to develop healthier perspectives on their professional experiences.

EMDR offers paramedics and EMTs an innovative and specific intervention for trauma. Through the exploration of traumatic memories with eye movement therapy, EMDR facilitates a healing journey that not only lessens the emotional impact but also encourages a fundamental reorganization of cognitive and emotional frameworks related to these experiences. This can lead to improved psychological well-being and resilience for paramedics and EMTs as they navigate the challenges of their demanding profession.

Group Therapy:

Group therapy for paramedics and emergency medical technicians (EMTs) offers a valuable therapeutic avenue tailored to their unique challenges as healthcare professionals. In this intimate setting, healthcare workers find solace in the company of peers who deeply understand the realities of emergency medical services.

For paramedics and EMTs, group therapy is beneficial not just for sharing their stories, but also for expressing the emotional nuances of their profession. This sharing fosters mutual understanding, creating an environment of empathy and camaraderie. It provides a space for communicating fears, successes, challenges, and concerns, offering an opportunity to feel heard and validated in a way that might be challenging to find elsewhere.

Moreover, the group dynamic creates a strong sense of belonging, helping individuals realize they are not alone in navigating the complexities of their profession. This shared understanding can alleviate the sense of isolation that emergency responders often feel due to the nature of their job, providing comfort and unity that can be deeply therapeutic.

Beyond emotional support, group therapy also acts as a platform for skill development. Participants work together to develop and practice coping strategies specifically suited to the demands and stressors of their roles. Through exchanging coping mechanisms, resilience-boosting techniques, and practical insights, they enhance their ability to manage professional challenges more effectively.

Group therapy for paramedics and EMTs extends beyond traditional therapeutic models by offering a comprehensive approach to addressing the complex psychological and emotional aspects of emergency medical services. Through shared experiences, mutual support, and skill- building exercises, this form of therapy becomes an invaluable resource for those dedicated to saving lives, while also nurturing their own resilience.

Mindfulness-Based Stress Reduction (MBSR):

Mindfulness-based stress reduction (MBSR) is a therapeutic framework designed to immerse individuals in the present moment, enhancing awareness of thoughts and emotions. For paramedics and Emergency Medical Technicians (EMTs) in emergency medical services, who often face high-pressure situations requiring quick decisions, mindfulness offers an effective coping strategy.

At its core, MBSR helps paramedics and EMTs navigate their professional challenges by fostering a keen yet nonjudgmental awareness of their mental and emotional states. This practice encourages them to observe their cognitive and emotional responses without self-criticism, laying the foundation for deeper understanding of their psychological reactions. For emergency medical services personnel, MBSR is a valuable tool for managing the inherent stress and anxiety of their roles.

Mindfulness equips emergency response professionals with a vital psychological framework for effective operation. By practicing presence in chaotic situations, first responders develop the ability to make objective decisions under pressure. Nonjudgmental observation helps them process stress differently, leading to healthier coping mechanisms beyond the immediate demands of their job.

MBSR fosters emotional resilience among paramedics and EMTs. It promotes recognition of shared experiences and emotional challenges within a supportive environment, helping to alleviate the isolation often felt in this profession. Group-based mindfulness exercises foster camaraderie and understanding, allowing for open discussions about the psychological impacts of their work.

Recognized as an effective therapeutic approach, MBSR offers paramedics and EMTs a path toward increased self-awareness, better stress management, and enhanced emotional resilience. By adopting mindfulness principles, first responders not only strengthen their ability to handle the demands of their careers in emergency medical services but also contribute to more sustainable career paths in this field.

Evidenced-Based Medication Management:

Evidence-based medication management (EBMM) is a key aspect of therapy for paramedics and emergency medical technicians (EMTs), especially in treating mental health conditions like posttraumatic stress disorder (PTSD). EBMM combines understanding of both physiological and psychological factors, allowing paramedics and EMTs to deliver care in a systematic, evidence- driven manner.

Within this therapeutic framework, medication introduction and adjustment are guided by thorough evaluations conducted by psychiatric professionals. For emergency response teams like paramedics and EMTs, collaboration with psychiatrists or psychiatric nurse practitioners is vital. These specialists assess an individual's mental health by examining symptom severity and nature, medical history, and potential interactions between medications or with existing physiological conditions.

In EBMM, prescribing medication involves more than addressing symptoms; it focuses on holistic well-being. Medication choices are made based on empirical evidence and individual needs, recognizing the specific challenges faced by paramedics and EMTs in their demanding roles.

EBMM extends beyond mere medication dispensation; it encompasses continuous evaluation of each patient's response to prescribed drugs, regular follow-ups, and collaborative communication between healthcare providers and emergency responders. This dynamic approach allows for timely adjustments to medication regimens to cater to the evolving needs of individuals.

For paramedics and EMTs, EBMM is more than conventional pharmacological intervention it's an integrative, multidimensional strategy. It combines evidence-based medication practices with a deep understanding of the challenges faced by emergency responders. This approach aims to alleviate distressing symptoms, build resilience, and enhance overall psychological well- being. Through this comprehensive method, paramedics and EMTs receive support in managing mental health conditions effectively while maintaining their own mental stability.

Critical Incident Stress Management (CISM) and Critical Incident Response (CIR):

Critical incident stress management (CISM) and critical incident response (CIR) both play vital roles in supporting the mental and emotional well-being of paramedics and emergency medical technicians (EMTs), often encounter high-stress situations in their line of work. Given their exposure to traumatic incidents, these tailored therapeutic methodologies are essential for mitigating both immediate and long-term psychological effects.

CISM employs a proactive and preventative approach, focusing on early intervention to reduce the impact of traumatic events. This method is particularly beneficial for paramedics and EMTs who frequently face extremely distressing scenes. CISM offers a structured framework for processing these experiences, including debriefing sessions, facilitated discussions, and educational modules to help normalize and understand their responses to stress.

CIR addresses the aftermath of critical incidents, focusing on the need for ongoing support. It recognizes that the effects of such incidents may emerge over time, potentially affecting a individual's well-being. CIR involves intensive, sustained interventions, providing paramedics and EMTs with resources like regular follow-up appointments, counseling services, and peer support groups, which cultivate a sense of community among emergency responders.

Both CISM and CIR emphasize the importance of peer support, acknowledging the value of empathy and guidance from those with similar experiences. Creating safe spaces for paramedics and EMTs to share their thoughts and emotions without judgment is key to these approaches. Additionally, they incorporate stress management education, resilience-building exercises, and self-care practices to further support emergency responders' mental well-being.

CISM and CIR are indispensable in addressing the challenges faced by paramedics and EMTs. By combining proactive measures with ongoing support and education, these methodologies significantly contribute to the mental and emotional health of those who dedicate their lives to saving others. As emergency response services evolve, the integration of CISM and CIR will be increasingly vital in fostering resilience and supportive communities among paramedics and EMTs.

Conclusion:

Paramedics and emergency medical technicians (EMTs) serve on the front lines of healthcare, saving lives with unwavering commitment but bearing an immense emotional toll as a result. While their commitment is undeniable, mental wellness may suffer as a result. This research into therapeutic interventions for paramedics and EMTs has shed light on the specific mental health challenges they face, including trauma and post-traumatic stress disorder (PTSD), and explores tailored therapeutic approaches for their unique needs.

Professional therapeutic interventions such as cognitive-behavioral therapies and trauma- focused treatments are a necessity for paramedics and EMTs. These approaches do more than alleviate symptoms; they guide these professionals towards psychological resilience and sustainable mental well-being strategies. With these effective therapeutic techniques, paramedics and EMTs can better manage the challenges associated with their demanding profession, not only recovering but also strengthening their psychological equilibrium.

| 7 |

Chapter 6: Mental Health Therapy for Dispatchers and 911 Operators

The Hidden Trauma of Dispatchers and 911 Operator

Emergency response is unpredictable and high-stakes, with dispatchers and 911 operators at its core, linking those in distress to first responders. This subchapter uncovers a hidden aspect of their roles: the significant, often lifelong trauma they endure. Beneath their essential duties lies a depth of psychological stressors, which, if left unaddressed, can severely impact their mental well-being. This section examines the daily experiences of trauma faced by dispatchers and 911 operators and the challenges they confront in their roles.

These professionals regularly deal with distressing scenarios that put their mental health at risk. From handling life-threatening emergencies to processing heartbreaking calls, they must make quick decisions that can have lasting impacts on their mental well-being, a facet of their work that often goes unrecognized.

We will explore the often-overlooked trauma manifestations, focusing on post traumatic stress disorder (PTSD). Beyond responding to immediate distressing events, dispatchers and 911 operators experience cumulative effects that impact heir professional and personal lives, with profound ramifications on their relationships and overall psychological health.

At the heart of addressing this trauma is the indispensable role of mental health therapy, particularly when tailored to the unique challenges of dispatchers and 911 operators. By fostering an environment where seeking mental health support is stigma-free, emergency response communities can build resilience and mitigate the long-term consequences of trauma.

This narrative serves as a call to action, advocating for a more inclusive and considerate approach to the mental health of dispatchers and 911 operators. Highlighting their hidden trauma and advocating for therapeutic solutions, this subchapter aims to raise awareness and spark positive change for these vital figures in emergency response.

The Unseen Toll:

Emergency dispatchers and 911 operators play an often-understated role in emergency response, constantly immersed in the chaos of human crises. As the first point of contact for those in crisis, they are exposed to a relentless stream of trauma via phone calls. Handling callers' intense emotions like panic, fear, and despair, while maintaining composure, places a significant psychological burden on these professionals, further intensified by the chaotic nature of their work environment.

Constant exposure to distressing situations poses a grave danger to dispatchers and 911 operators' mental well-being, increasing their risk for post-traumatic stress disorder (PTSD), anxiety disorders, depression, and other trauma-related reactions. It's not just individual incidents that impact their mental health; the cumulative effect of daily emotional challenges also takes a toll.

Diving more deeply into the mental health challenges faced by these professionals, it becomes evident that their suffering extends beyond the immediate aftermath of distressing calls. The emotional aftermath of such experiences often seeps into their personal lives, affecting their overall sense of well-being. The constant exposure to human suffering can lead to hypervigilance, making it difficult for dispatchers and operators to relax and detach from their emotionally demanding roles.

Emergency dispatch work comes with its own set of stressors that often go unacknowledged, further compounding difficulty in seeking the necessary support. Stigmatization and cultures that downplay their emotional toll can hinder access to mental health resources. Therefore, addressing their mental health needs requires an interdisciplinary approach, encompassing both therapeutic interventions and systemic changes within the profession.

Mental health therapy tailored specifically towards emergency dispatchers and 911 operators must be prioritized if we want them to remain psychologically resilient. This includes targeted counseling sessions that address their unique challenges and provide safe spaces for processing the emotional burden of their experiences. Additionally, preventative measures like regular mental health check-ins, peer support programs, and coping strategy education can help build a resilient mental health framework for this community.

Overall, the mental health challenges faced by dispatchers and 911 operators go beyond handling distress calls, affecting their daily lives and overall well-being. Recognizing the specific needs of their profession and providing comprehensive mental health support systems are crucial steps in protecting the mental health of these vital members of emergency response services.

Unique Challenges:

Dispatchers and 911 operators face distinct challenges in their roles, setting them apart from other first responders. While they're not physically at emergency scenes, they become emotionally entangled in the incidents they manage. Unlike first responders who witness events firsthand, dispatchers and operators navigate distressing situations through verbal communication alone, creating vivid mental images from auditory information. This can intensify the emotional impact of each call.

The psychological strain on dispatchers and 911 operators is often compounded by the inherent lack of closure in their profession. Unlike frontline workers who see emergency responses unfold, dispatchers are frequently left without knowledge of how crises resolve, leading to feelings of helplessness and uncertainty about the outcomes of their efforts.

This unique combination of factors results in a specific form of occupational stress for dispatchers and 911 operators, characterized by unresolved trauma and emotional exhaustion. Their job requires constant vigilance, making it challenging to detach from the emotional impact of calls. Over time, this can heighten their risk for mental health issues like anxiety, depression, and PTSD.

Tailored mental health therapy for dispatchers and 911 operators has become essential. Effective interventions should address the auditory nature of their work, the lack of closure, and the cumulative impact on their mental well-being. Techniques could include cognitive-behavioral therapy to reframe distressing thoughts, mindfulness practices for acute stress management, and psychoeducation for resilience and coping strategies.

Emergency communication centers must create a stigma-free environment to promote mental health awareness and encourage the pursuit of professional assistance without fear of judgment. Implementing debriefing sessions, peer support programs, and providing access to mental health professionals can enhance the well-being of dispatchers and 911 operators. Recognizing their unique challenges and offering targeted mental health interventions are essential steps in supporting these critical players in emergency management.

Recognizing the Signs:

Navigating the complex world of mental health therapy for dispatchers and 911 operators requires an in-depth knowledge of their specific challenges, often taking on emergency roles where distressing incidents may arise daily. To successfully provide therapeutic support to these professionals is not indicative of weakness but instead represents an act of courage and self-care.

Trauma symptoms can manifest in various ways for dispatchers and 911 operators. Intrusive memories from emergency calls might linger, affecting their daily lives. Nightmares may replay distressing scenes, disrupting sleep. The mental strain from their demanding roles can impair concentration and cognitive functions. Cumulative stress might lead to irritability, straining interpersonal relationships, and impacting overall mental health. Emotional numbing can develop as a coping mechanism, allowing them to function professionally but potentially leading to emotional disconnection.

Proactively acknowledging and understanding these signs is an important first step towards healing for dispatchers and 911 operators. This recognition is an act of resilience and underscores the importance of comprehensive mental health support within emergency response organizations. Tailored therapeutic interventions can help these professionals manage the emotional complexities of their roles, fostering a resilient workforce better equipped to serve the community in times of crisis.

The Importance of Mental Health Therapy:

Comprehensive mental health therapy tailored for dispatchers and 911 operators is crucial in addressing the unique challenges of their high-pressure profession. These individuals, as first responders in emergencies, encounter intense stressors and potentially traumatic experiences, handling life-or-death situations. Therapy focused on first responders provides a space where dispatchers and operators can openly express their emotions.

In this specialized therapy setting, therapists explore beyond just surface-level stressors. They delve into the daily experiences of dispatchers and 911 operators, helping them unpack the emotional toll of managing emergency calls, coordinating responses, and dealing with the unpredictability of their roles.

Customized therapy offers a supportive framework for developing healthy coping mechanisms, specifically designed for the unique challenges faced by dispatchers and operators. This includes strategies to manage acute stress, regulate emotional responses, and build resilience against prolonged exposure to distressing incidents. Therapists also help them recognize and mitigate the impacts of cumulative trauma exposure to prevent compassion fatigue or burnout.

This specialized mental health intervention focuses on the hidden trauma that comes from repeatedly handling crises and high-pressure situations. Therapists work collaboratively with dispatchers and operators to identify and address latent emotional distress, creating an environment conducive to overcoming its effects and fostering healing.

By specifically tailoring mental health therapy to their needs, professionals in this field not only address immediate well-being but also build resilience and mental health for those essential to public safety. This approach acknowledges their significant contributions and aims to ensure sustainable and healthy careers in the challenging yet essential field of emergency response.

Healing and Rebuilding:

Mental health therapy plays an essential part in improving dispatchers' and 911 operators' well- being, offering them a toolkit to deal with their unique challenges in this demanding profession.Therapy goes beyond providing stress management techniques - it serves as a transformative space where these professionals can explore deeper parts of themselves psychologically.

Therapy interventions for dispatchers and 911 operators take an integrative approach, considering both immediate and chronic stresses associated with emergency response work, as well as any emotional intricacies that might emerge over time. Therapies go beyond surface-level stress management by equipping individuals with personalized strategies for effectively regulating emotions - such as cultivating emotional intelligence, increasing self-awareness, and creating tailored coping mechanisms designed specifically for the high-pressure environments commonplace within emergency response work environments.

Therapy provides dispatchers and 911 operators a vital outlet to express their experiences to people who understand their unique challenges. Through therapy sessions, these professionals find comfort in having someone validate their experiences while creating an atmosphere of compassion that extends beyond individual therapy sessions into an extended network of first responders who face similar difficulties.

Therapeutic interventions also play an essential part in developing resilience among dispatchers and 911 operators. By exploring sources of stressors, addressing emotional triggers, and devising coping mechanisms for themselves, individuals can strengthen psychological resilience; not only to deal with immediate challenges but to also deal with prolonged exposure to intense situations.

Therapy offers a proactive solution for mental health by encouraging self-care and preventing more severe mental conditions from emerging. By creating an environment of psychological well-being through therapy sessions, dispatchers and 911 operators can prioritize their mental well-being without facing the stigma associated with seeking support in high-pressure professions.

Mental health therapy for dispatchers and 911 operators goes beyond traditional stress management practices; it provides an intensive journey that explores psychological experiences, encourages community connections, and builds resilience. By immersing themselves in this journey, these professionals not only enhance their ability to manage stress more effectively but also lay the groundwork for sustained mental well-being in an otherwise stressful field such as emergency response.

Conclusion

Mental health therapy is a vital tool for dispatchers and 911 operators, offering them a means to deal with the unique challenges of their demanding profession. This therapy extends beyond stress management, providing a transformative space for these professionals to explore their psychological experiences.

In therapy, dispatchers and 911 operators confront both the immediate and chronic stresses associated with their work in emergency response, as well as the emotional complexities that emerge over time. Therapies are designed to equip them with strategies for effectively regulating emotions, enhancing emotional intelligence, self-awareness, and developing coping mechanisms specifically for the pressures of their work environment.

This therapy provides dispatchers and 911 operators with an outlet to express and process their experiences with professionals who understand their unique challenges. In therapy sessions, they find validation and support, fostering a compassionate environment that extends beyond the individual sessions.

These therapeutic interventions are essential in building resilience among dispatchers and 911 operators. By addressing sources of stress, emotional triggers, and creating coping strategies, these professionals can strengthen their psychological resilience, preparing them to handle both the immediate and long-term challenges of their roles.

Mental health therapy for dispatchers and 911 operators is more than just traditional stress management; it's an in-depth journey that acknowledges and addresses the psychological intricacies of their roles in emergency response. By engaging in this therapeutic process, they enhance their ability to manage stress and build a foundation for long-term mental well-being.

Breaking the Silence: Encouraging Help-Seeking Behavior

911 operators and dispatchers play an indispensable yet often unnoticed role in first responder duties, continuously exposed to trauma-inducing events. This exposure often results in psychological strain such as post-traumatic stress disorder (PTSD). Being on the front lines

of emergency response, they are near distressful situations that threaten public safety; constant exposure to violence often leaves 911 operators and dispatchers vulnerable to emotional distress and isolation - essential roles indeed!

Mental health therapy for 911 operators and dispatchers must acknowledge the unique challenges inherent to their occupation. Unlike other first responders, dispatchers manage crises from an invisible vantage point, witnessing heartbreaking incidents without the power to intervene directly, which significantly increases emotional strain. These special circumstances necessitate a tailored therapeutic approach, recognizing the psychological toll of their responsibilities.

Breaking the silence on mental health within the 911 operator and dispatcher community is an integral part of fostering a wellness culture. This requires acknowledging their strength and resilience and dispelling the misconception that seeking mental health assistance denotes weakness. In fact, pursuing help should be viewed as a brave step towards healing and fortitude.

Emphasizing the need for therapeutic interventions tailored to the specific stressors and emotional challenges of 911 operators and dispatchers is vital for their mental well-being. Encouraging a culture that supports seeking help not only recognizes their psychological complexities but also bolsters their resilience, which is essential for public safety.

Dispatchers and 911 operators are key in emergency response, often handling high-stress situations with professionalism. However, exposure to distressing events can impact their mental health, despite their resilience. The prevalent culture in their field often overlooks the importance of addressing psychological well-being.

Mental health therapy for dispatchers and 911 operators extends far beyond simple awareness of their vulnerabilities. Instead, it involves an intricate understanding of their daily experiences, the cumulative impact of being exposed to emergencies, and its long-term ramifications on mental health. Listening to distressing calls, making quick decisions under duress, and handling life-or-death scenarios can cause immense stress for operators, creating mental anguish that often outlives physical ailments.

Recognizing the need for therapy is a sign of strength and self-awareness. Therapy provides a confidential space for dispatchers and 911 operators to explore the emotional complexities unique to their roles. Tailored therapeutic interventions, like cognitive-behavioral therapy (CBT), trauma-focused therapy, and mindfulness techniques, are beneficial. They help manage stress, build resilience, and develop healthy coping mechanisms, mitigating long-term exposure effects.

By engaging in mental health therapy, dispatchers and 911 operators not only prioritize their well-being but also enhance their effectiveness in protecting communities. Therapy builds emotional resilience, maintains peak performance under pressure, and fosters sustainable practices in their demanding profession, ultimately contributing to improved public safety and well-being. Cultivating an environment that encourages support strengthens first-responder communities, leading to better public safety and collective well-being.

Mental health therapy for dispatchers and 911 operators requires a comprehensive approach. Encouraging help-seeking behaviors involves strategies tailored to their specific challenges. Normalizing therapy is key to combating mental health stigma in emergency response, involving sharing success stories and discussing diverse experiences within first responder communities. Acknowledging differing manifestations of mental illness challenges while showing various therapeutic journeys can create relatability among individuals while dispelling misconceptions.

Educating about therapy's benefits requires exploring its complexities, highlighting its contributions to well-being, interpersonal relationships, and job performance. This clarifies that seeking therapy is a proactive step towards holistic self-improvement. Tailoring resources to the unique needs of dispatchers and 911 operators involves providing access to specialized therapists and support groups, understanding their specific stressors to offer targeted assistance. This empowers individuals on their mental well-being journey.

Establishing an open workplace culture requires deeply examining its dynamics. It's important to cultivate an environment where discussions about mental health are encouraged and actively supported. This means dismantling long-standing norms, implementing policies to protect individuals from judgment or repercussions, and promoting leadership that embodies empathy and understanding. Achieving a cultural shift towards de-stigmatizing mental health issues can be accomplished through continuous initiatives, training courses, and integrating mental health awareness into the organizational ethos.

Mental health therapy for dispatchers and 911 necessitates a deep dive into their unique experiences. This involves dismantling stigma through relatable narratives, highlighting specific benefits of therapy, tailoring resources to meet their needs, and fostering an open workplace culture where openness and support are paramount. Only through a holistic and nuanced strategy can we successfully address their mental health needs.

Entering the realm of mental health therapy for dispatchers and 911 operators requires acknowledging the unique challenges and stressors inherent to their profession. They regularly face high-pressure situations and witness traumatizing events that can have lasting psychological effects. Embracing a culture that encourages help-seeking behavior goes beyond acknowledging support; it involves an inclusive approach to eliminate the stigma associated with mental health struggles, enabling true rehabilitation.

Attaining mental well-being for dispatchers and 911 operators involves employing customized therapy techniques tailored to their experiences. These therapies should address not only the immediate impacts of trauma but also the chronic stress and emotional strain they face over time. Therapeutic interventions can include cognitive-behavioral therapy, eye movement desensitization and reprocessing (EMDR), and mindfulness-based stress reduction approaches, among others.

Establishing a supportive community for dispatchers and 911 operators requires collaborative efforts from professionals, peers, supervisors, and leadership. It's important to create an environment that normalizes seeking help and emphasizes emotional well-being. Training programs and awareness campaigns play a vital role in this, spreading information about mental health resources, fostering empathy, and dispelling myths that seeking assistance shows weakness.

We aim to empower dispatchers and 911 operators to acknowledge the importance of mental health and actively pursue resilience and recovery. Providing access to specialized interventions and breaking down barriers to therapy are essential in fostering a resilient and mentally healthy first responder community. Recognizing the significant impact their work has on mental well being and nurturing a supportive environment are key to sustained healing and strength recuperation. Seeking help is a step towards individual recovery and a way to change the narrative around mental health in emergency response professions.

Dispatchers and 911 operators play an invaluable role within emergency response systems, shouldering the responsibility for managing critical situations amidst chaos. Their daily lives often entail delicate negotiations on a precarious edge balancing high-stress scenarios where quick, impactful decisions are necessary. Regular encounters with emergencies, accidents, and distressful situations increase their risk of developing conditions like PTSD.

The complex roles of dispatchers and 911 operators necessitate custom-tailored mental health support. Conventional therapy methods might not address all the unique challenges of their profession, leading to the development of specialized therapy approaches. These approaches acknowledge the multiple pressures they face, such as handling intense emergency calls and the emotional impact of daily exposure to critical situations.

Mental health therapy for dispatchers and 911 operators focuses on building resilience and coping mechanisms specifically designed for their job demands. Collaborating with therapists, these professionals develop strategies to promote emotional regulation, stress resilience, and effective coping skills. Therapy sessions also address vicarious trauma and the mental strain resulting from constant exposure to emergencies.

An important component of therapy for frontline responders like dispatchers and 911 operators is creating a safe and confidential space for them to express and process their emotions freely. Due to the nature of their work with confidential emergencies, these professionals often internalize emotional stress, making it essential to have an outlet for expression. Therapists use evidence-based techniques to help articulate emotions, fostering an environment where dispatchers and 911 operators can comfortably discuss their challenges without fear of judgment.

Mindfulness and relaxation techniques have become integral in mental health therapy for professionals in high-stress jobs. For dispatchers and 911 operators, who require constant acute focus and rapid decision-making, integrating these practices helps mitigate chronic stress and improve overall well-being. Therapists support them through exercises like mindfulness and breathing techniques, promoting emotional balance and helping prevent burnout.

Mental health therapy tailored specifically for dispatchers and 911 operators extends beyond traditional approaches, acknowledging the unique aspects of their work environment and its effects on well-being. Providing the necessary support to handle the daily challenges encountered in emergency response systems, this specialized therapy is key in offering assistance while fostering resilience and longevity among these essential contributors to emergency response systems.

Cognitive Behavioral Therapy (CBT)

Cognitive behavioral therapy (CBT) can be a transformative therapeutic approach for dispatchers and 911 operators, who frequently encounter high-stress situations in their roles. CBT, focusing on the interplay between thoughts, emotions, and behaviors, is particularly beneficial for emergency responders dealing with such intense work environments. CBT can be transformative!

CBT involves a detailed examination of thought patterns that contribute to distress or negative emotional states. For dispatchers, this could mean addressing repetitive thoughts linked to trauma-inducing incidents, feelings of helplessness, or an overwhelming sense of responsibility. The therapeutic process of CBT helps these professionals identify and challenge negative thoughts, providing a structured approach to reframe these thoughts more constructively.

For dispatchers, CBT extends beyond basic coping mechanisms. It teaches practical skills to actively alter cognitive processes in real-time, fostering resilience and adaptability to ongoing stressors. This might involve developing more balanced views of their roles, accepting the limitations in crisis situations, or prioritizing emotional well-being.

CBT also helps dispatchers develop coping strategies tailored to the unique demands of their job. This could include techniques like positive self-talk, mindfulness practices, or establishing healthy boundaries between work and personal life. These skills aid in enhancing emotional regulation and maintaining psychological stability during tough incidents.

CBT offers dispatchers and 911 operators a dynamic and tailored approach to mental health therapy. It goes beyond treating stress and trauma symptoms, actively engaging with thought processes that influence emotional responses. With tools for cognitive restructuring and emotional regulation, CBT equips these emergency responders to better navigate their complex roles with increased resilience, self-awareness, and well-being.

Eye Movement Desensitization and Reprocessing (EMDR)

EMDR therapy has proven itself as a highly effective tool for individuals, including dispatchers and 911 operators, in processing and recovering from traumatic memories. This therapy is based on bilateral stimulation, engaging both sides of the brain through eye movements, following moving lights, or rhythmic tapping.

A significant advantage of EMDR is its ability to facilitate adaptive information processing. Traumatic memories are often stored in a way that hinders integration into one's memory network. EMDR helps reprocess these memories more adaptively, reducing their emotional intensity. This is particularly beneficial for dispatchers and 911 operators who regularly encounter emotionally challenging incidents.

EMDR therapy involves several stages. Initially, the therapist works with the individual to identify specific distressing memories, like critical incidents or impactful calls. Then, bilateral stimulation techniques, such as following hand movements or auditory tones, are used while the individual recalls these memories.

During bilateral stimulation, cognitive processing is enhanced, allowing individuals to reassess traumatic memories more adaptively, often leading to reduced emotional distress and a greater sense of resolution. Over multiple EMDR sessions, individuals typically experience a decrease in the intensity of their reactions, gaining better control over their emotional responses.

For dispatchers and 911 operators who frequently work in high-stress environments, EMDR can be an invaluable tool in managing the emotional toll of their work. By processing past traumatic memories, EMDR aids in improving mental resilience and adaptability, contributing to overall well-being. Additionally, its versatility allows EMDR to be seamlessly integrated into broader therapeutic plans, complementing other mental health treatment techniques.

Mindfulness-based stress reduction (MBSR)

Mindfulness-based stress reduction (MBSR), offers considerable advantages for professionals like dispatchers and 911 operators working in stressful environments. MBSR, a well-established therapeutic approach, encourages these professionals to practice present-moment awareness and nonjudgmental acceptance of their thoughts and emotions, particularly useful in the high- pressure situations they frequently encounter.

This mindfulness practice helps dispatchers and 911 operators cultivate an awareness of the present moment, enhancing their focus and acute awareness of both their surroundings and internal experiences.

By acknowledging thoughts without judgment, mindfulness enables them to maintain objective decision-making, even in intense situations. This increased self-awareness also aids in emotional regulation, allowing them to navigate demanding scenarios with greater composure.

MBSR provides techniques for staying centered amidst chaos. It teaches dispatchers and 911 operators to keep their focus on the present moment, preventing them from getting overwhelmed by past or future concerns. This skill not only improves their performance in emergency situations but can also help reduce long-term stress levels.

Integrating MBSR into their mental health therapy involves guided meditation, body scans, and mindful breathing exercises. These methods are designed to promote relaxation, improve concentration, and create a non-reactive awareness of thoughts and emotions. As dispatchers and operators incorporate these techniques into their daily routines, they may experience enhanced stress management, leading to improvements in their mental health and overall job satisfaction.

MBSR's flexibility allows it to be specifically tailored to the unique stressors faced by dispatchers and 911 operators, offering an effective and personalized approach to enhancing the well-being of these essential emergency response professionals.

Group Therapy, Critical Incident Stress Management (CISM), and Critical Incident Response (CIR)

Group approaches like group therapy, critical incident stress management (CISM), and critical incident response (CIR) play an invaluable role in supporting the well-being of dispatchers and 911 operators. Group therapy offers a space where they can connect with peers who share similar experiences. This connection is vital in an environment like dispatching, which can often feel isolating. In group sessions, participants find validation, support, and understanding, and can freely express their thoughts and emotions without judgment.

Group therapy allows dispatchers and 911 operators to exchange coping strategies, aiding each other in managing stress, building resilience, and handling the emotional toll of their work. The collaborative learning environment also fosters camaraderie among participants, reinforcing that they are not alone in their daily struggles.

Critical incident stress management (CISM is a specialized approach tailored for emergency responders. It involves a structured process to assist individuals in coping with the emotional aftermath of critical incidents, recognizing that trauma exposure can have lasting effects on mental health and aiming to mitigate any negative long-term impacts.

Critical incident response (CIR) expands support by providing immediate and coordinated responses to critical incidents. CIR understands the importance of timely intervention, acknowledging that effectively addressing trauma events promptly can mitigate their impact. This approach can include debriefing sessions, educational components, and ongoing support to ensure the mental well-being of dispatchers and 911 operators.

Mental health therapy approaches for dispatchers and 911 operators span a spectrum of strategies, from group therapy, Critical Incident Stress Management (CISM), and Critical Incident Response (CIR), to provide essential support. These approaches also foster a sense of community among professionals facing unique challenges in their roles, ultimately strengthening their resilience. By exploring such techniques further, dispatchers and 911 operators can more comprehensively address their mental health needs and increase their resilience to the unavoidable stressors of their occupations.

Trauma-Focused Cognitive Behavioral Therapy (TF-CBT),

Trauma-focused cognitive behavioral therapy (TF-CBT) stands as an invaluable and tailored therapeutic solution to address the unique challenges experienced by dispatchers and 911 operators in their pivotal roles in emergency response. As an established evidence-based intervention, TF-CBT reveals complex trauma dynamics while offering professional tools necessary for handling these high-stress occupations.

At its core, TF-CBT for dispatchers and 911 operators is carefully tailored to address the subtle psychological repercussions associated with repeated exposure to distressing and traumatic incidents. Going beyond conventional interventions, this therapy offers targeted strategies to address trauma-related symptoms. It helps professionals acknowledge traumatic events and engage in skill-building exercises to enhance their coping mechanisms.

In TF-CBT, dispatchers and operators embark on a structured therapeutic journey aimed at alleviating the distressing effects of traumatic experiences. This process involves understanding the psychological impact of their roles, validating emotions linked to their experiences, and building resilience against the ongoing challenges in emergency response work.

The approach combines psychoeducation, cognitive restructuring, and specific techniques designed for dispatchers and 911 operators. Psychoeducation is key to understanding trauma's impact on mental health. Through cognitive restructuring, TF-CBT assists in reframing negative thought patterns and promotes adaptive coping strategies, enabling these professionals to maintain control even in chaotic situations.

TF-CBT also focuses on the cumulative impact of constant exposure to distressing incidents, emphasizing the importance of ongoing support and self-care practices. This comprehensive approach not only eases current symptoms but also aims to strengthen the long-term mental well-being and resilience of dispatchers and 911 operators in their demanding professions. Ultimately, TF-CBT offers profound and lasting positive changes in mental health and resilience for those crucial to public safety and emergency response.

Conclusion:

Dispatchers and 911 operators, as first responders, often witness horrific incidents that can lead to lasting psychological impacts like posttraumatic stress disorder (PTSD). To address their complex mental health needs, a variety of therapeutic approaches prove invaluable.

Cognitive behavioral therapy (CBT) is particularly beneficial for dispatchers and 911 operators. It enables them to reassess distressing incidents more objectively and develop adaptive coping mechanisms, enhancing their resilience. Eye movement desensitization and reprocessing (EMDR) is also effective, specifically targeting the processing of traumatic memories to reduce
their emotional intensity.

Mindfulness-based stress reduction (MBSR) provides an innovative way for dispatchers and 911 operators to build resilience. This approach, focusing on present-moment awareness, enhances emotional regulation skills and helps manage cumulative workplace stress.

Group therapy is an invaluable modality, creating an inclusive community where shared experiences can be freely discussed. It reduces feelings of isolation and reinforces a collective commitment to mental wellness, making it an essential modality for dispatchers and 911 operators.

Trauma-focused therapy, tailored to the unique demands of emergency response work, is crucial. This specialized approach allows dispatchers and 911 operators to process and heal from the job-related trauma, addressing all aspects of their experiences.

Implementation of multiple therapeutic techniques such as cognitive behavior therapy (CBT), EMDR, MBSR, group therapy, and trauma-focused therapy is a powerful and comprehensive strategy to bolster dispatchers and 911 operators' mental well-being. These approaches provide the necessary tools for them to handle emotional challenges associated with their roles and flourish as key contributors of emergency response systems.

| **8** |

Chapter 7: Holistic Approaches to Mental Health Therapy for First Responders

Incorporating Mindfulness and Meditation Practices

First responders often face immense stress, making finding inner tranquility challenging. However, mindfulness and meditation practices have proven to be effective methods for alleviating trauma reactions and post-traumatic stress disorder (PTSD).

Mindfulness involves paying attention to each moment without judgment, with a deep awareness of thoughts, emotions, and bodily sensations, leading to increased self-awareness. Mastery of mindfulness allows individuals to approach stressful situations with calm confidence, providing a way to navigate challenges in their professional lives.

Meditation, on the other hand, is a deliberate technique to train the mind and induce deep relaxation. It involves focused attention and quieting the constant stream of thoughts that can trigger stress and anxiety. Meditation can be transformative, alleviating symptoms associated with PTSD such as hypervigilance, intrusive thoughts, and disrupted sleep patterns. With regular practice, it can be instrumental in treating these symptoms.

Starting mindfulness and meditation practices can be simple and does not require much time. It begins with setting aside a few minutes each day in a quiet space, closing the eyes, taking deep breaths, and focusing on the sensations of breathing. This foundational practice strengthens concentration and resilience over time.

Infusing mindfulness into daily activities extends its benefits beyond formal meditation sessions. Practicing mindfulness while driving, eating, or doing household chores, by fully engaging with the present moment and its sensory experiences, fosters groundedness and stress relief.

Mindfulness and meditation complement other treatment modalities like cognitive behavioral therapy (CBT) or eye movement desensitization and reprocessing (EMDR) in mental health therapy. They provide powerful tools for stress management, emotional regulation, and building resilience during adversity.

Healing from trauma reactions and PTSD is a gradual process, with mindfulness and meditation serving as key components. This journey requires time and personalized adaptation. Prioritizing mental health practices is an essential step toward recovery, reclaiming control, and revitalizing lives.

The Role of Physical Exercise in Mental Health Recovery

First responders, facing demanding and high-stress environments, are often exposed to traumatic experiences that may lead to conditions like post-traumatic stress disorder (PTSD). Physical exercise emerges as an effective tool for managing this trauma and aiding in recovery.

Regular physical exercise releases endorphins, providing biochemical and psychological benefits. Activities like running or weightlifting offer first responders a tangible outlet for stress, channeling it towards physical exertion rather than mental concentration. This not only helps in immediate tension release but also builds long-term resilience against stressors by engaging in challenging physical exercises.

Physical exercise significantly improves sleep quality, a crucial aspect of mental health for first responders. Regular activities like yoga or swimming help regulate circadian rhythms and have a calming effect on the nervous system. This leads to better sleep hygiene and emotional resilience, as sleep is crucial for the brain to consolidate emotions and experiences into memories. Exercise thus contributes to building resilient minds and spirits, enhancing overall emotional well-being.

Exercise provides a sense of empowerment that transcends immediate physiological benefits. It allows first responders to reclaim control over their body and mind, crucial when faced with situations that can induce feelings of helplessness. This sense of empowerment also extends into daily life, affecting how they perceive and respond to stressors both at work and beyond.

Physical activities tailored for first responders offer physical benefits and social support. Engaging in team sports or group fitness classes fosters camaraderie and shared experiences, providing additional resilience as they find comfort in their peers' understanding and encouragement while dealing with trauma reactions or PTSD.

Mental health professionals recognize the importance of physical exercise in therapy for first responders. Tailoring interventions to individual needs, this may include setting fitness goals, incorporating exercise into daily routines, or organizing group activities to build community spirit. The goal is a personalized approach that addresses specific challenges faced by first responders while supporting their journey towards mental well-being recovery.

Physical exercise is not just an additional therapy measure for first responders in mental health recovery; it is an integral component. It addresses the physiological, psychological, and social aspects of trauma, offering resilience and well-being for those dedicated to serving others selflessly.

Exploring Alternative Therapies for Traumatic Reactions and PTSD

First responders face an increased likelihood of encountering traumatic incidents and experiencing post-traumatic stress disorder (PTSD). Their profession often exposes them to life- threatening emergencies that leave an indelible mark on their mental well-being. While traditional therapeutic methods have proven helpful for some first responders, their unique circumstances often necessitate an intensive exploration of alternative therapies for strengthening psychological resilience.

As first responders undergo unprecedented stressors and experiences, it becomes imperative to explore innovative and tailored approaches that meet them on a personal level. Mindfulness-based techniques, emphasizing present-moment awareness and nonjudgmental acceptance, have proven highly successful at mitigating trauma symptoms. By cultivating increased self-awareness and emotional regulation, practices like mindfulness meditation or yoga can help first responders build resilient mindsets to minimize the impact on their wellbeing.

Art therapy offers another promising means for first responders to manage traumatic reactions. Recognizing creative expression as an effective therapeutic technique, art therapy provides an avenue for processing intense emotions without verbalization. By exploring various artistic mediums, individuals can externalize internal struggles while deepening their understanding of experiences through artistic exploration.

Animal-assisted therapy is an innovative and holistic solution in the battle to relieve post- traumatic stress. The companionship of specially trained therapy animals has been shown to decrease anxiety, promote relaxation, and boost overall well-being – especially useful for first responders facing intense situations.

As trauma in first responders is a complex problem, the investigation of alternative therapies must extend beyond traditional methods. Mindfulness practices, art therapy, and animal- assisted therapy represent promising avenues that warrant further study as possible sources of relief against trauma and PTSD. By adopting innovative approaches, these therapies could prove invaluable in creating psychological well-being tailored to first responder challenges.

Eye Movement Desensitization and Reprocessing (EMDR)

Eye movement desensitization and reprocessing (EMDR) is recognized as an evidence-based therapy approach, particularly beneficial for first responders processing traumatic memories. EMDR's core technique involves bilateral stimulation, which can be guided eye movements, tactile sensations, or auditory cues. This stimulation taps into the brain's natural information processing abilities to reprocess distressing memories, often contributing to post-traumatic stress disorder (PTSD) symptoms common among first responders.

A key element of EMDR for first responders is the precise targeting of traumatic memories. Therapists conduct thorough assessments to identify specific incidents that have left deep emotional scars. Once these memories are pinpointed, therapy includes various steps where bilateral stimulation is crucial. This stimulation can emulate the rapid eye movement (REM) phase of sleep, crucial for processing emotional experiences, helping first responders cope more effectively with traumatic events.

EMDR therapy also incorporates cognitive restructuring, using bilateral stimulation to examine and reevaluate thoughts, emotions, and beliefs linked to trauma. This process enables first responders to challenge and alter negative cognitions stemming from their experiences, fostering more balanced perspectives, and developing resilient coping mechanisms.

Desensitization is another primary component of EMDR, aimed at gradually reducing emotional reactions to traumatic memories. Bilateral stimulation aids in reorganizing these memories, making them less emotionally distressing over time. For first responders, this aspect of EMDR is particularly impactful, as it helps them maintain professional efficacy and emotional well-being despite repeated exposure to challenging situations.

Overall, EMDR offers first responders a sophisticated approach to trauma processing. Through bilateral stimulation and cognitive restructuring, this therapy provides a tailored and effective way for first responders to handle their traumatic experiences, enhancing their psychological resilience and overall well-being.

Equine-Assisted Therapy

Equine-assisted therapy (EAT) for first responders harnesses the enormous therapeutic potential of working with horses as a multifaceted approach to emotional well-being. These majestic animals, with their profound sensitivity and intuitive nature, create a safe space where individuals can explore their emotions without judgment from another human or horse; the therapeutic alliance between first responders and horses transcends traditional verbal therapies by tapping into nonverbal communication between human beings and these empathetic beings.

At the core of EAT is the ability of horses to mirror and respond to human emotions, providing first responders with reflective experiential learning. Interaction with horses gives insights into their own emotional states and behavioral patterns, as horses respond authentically and without judgment, reflecting the responder's feelings and actions.

Therapeutic use of horses offers first responders an invaluable aid in their journey towards greater self-awareness. They learn to recognize and regulate emotions, fostering emotional resilience and coping mechanisms. Engaging in activities like grooming, feeding, and direct interaction with horses, they form unique bonds that go beyond traditional therapy settings.

EAT also emphasizes mindfulness and presence. Engaging with horses, who are naturally attuned to being fully present due to their nature as prey animals, encourages first responders to be in the here and now, strengthening emotional regulation and stress management.

EAT offers first responders a unique form of stress relief through physical activity with horses. Direct interactions like leading, grooming, and riding provide an outlet for releasing tension and pent-up emotions. The rhythmic and repetitive nature of these activities promotes relaxation, which is particularly beneficial for first responders who regularly face challenging and demanding situations.

EAT for first responders is a holistic and dynamic approach to improving emotional well being. By leveraging the natural qualities of horses, this therapy transcends conventional methods, offering transformative experiences. These experiences are specifically tailored to address the complex emotional and psychological needs of those who are dedicated to serving and protecting others. Engaging in deeper connections with these majestic animals, first responders undergo journeys of self-discovery, emotional healing, and enhanced resilience.

Yoga and Mindfulness

Integrating yoga and mindfulness techniques into the lives of first responders is an effective strategy for reducing stress and anxiety, offering a holistic approach to mental and physical wellness. Research shows these practices have numerous benefits that go beyond the obvious.

Yoga is a valuable tool for first responders, helping them deal with unique challenges encountered in their careers. Synchronizing breath with movement in yoga enhances body awareness and control, boosting resilience in difficult situations. Incorporating poses focusing on flexibility, strength, and balance improves physical capabilities, aiding in injury prevention and overall fitness.

Mindfulness practices provide transformative tools for mental resilience. These practices cultivate present-moment awareness, crucial for first responders managing the relentless thoughts and emotions in high-stress situations. Techniques like mindful breathing, body scan meditations, or mindful walking help develop skills to remain grounded and focused amid chaos.

Beyond reducing stress, yoga and mindfulness improve sleep quality and emotional regulation. Regular practice helps first responders build emotional intelligence and strengthens interpersonal relationships within their teams. The relaxation response from yoga and mindfulness practices enhances sleep hygiene, allowing first responders to effectively recharge for the physical and mental demands of their work.

Yoga and mindfulness for first responders are more than just stress management tools; they form an integrated approach for cultivating mental and physical well-being, resilience, and improved performance in the demanding environments they navigate daily.

Art Therapy

Participating in creative expression through mediums like painting, drawing, or sculpting is a life-altering method for first responders engaged in art therapy. More than just crafting art, this therapy provides an outlet for exploring emotions without solely relying on verbal communication. Immersing in artistic processes such as painting or sculpting opens an effective means of self-expression, enabling first responders to navigate complex emotional landscapes without the constraints of traditional verbalization.

Art therapy, specifically tailored for first responders, becomes a tapestry where brush strokes or sculpting materials intertwine with a narrative of resilience and healing. This approach acknowledges their unique challenges and offers an expressive outlet beyond language barriers. Art becomes a refuge, aiding in reclaiming control over internal narratives and leading to profound empowerment.

Beyond its creation, art serves as a tangible representation of an individual's emotional journey, symbolizing resilience, strength, and the capacity for change. First responders can revisit and reinterpret their creations, facilitating deeper self-reflection and aiding in their post traumatic recovery.

Art therapists specializing in first responder care use art therapy as a means to explore traumas and stressors unique to the profession. The collaboration between the therapist and the responder provides a safe space to confront, process, and integrate experiences. Tailored art therapy emerges as an indispensable component in the support system for first responders, aiding in healing and self-discovery.

Wilderness Therapy

Wilderness therapy for first responders provides an immersive, therapeutic environment to reconnect with nature, offering profound healing effects that penetrate deep into their psyches. This approach transcends superficial touchpoints by immersing individuals in nature's embrace, surrounded by rustling leaves, fresh air, expansive landscapes, and dynamic self-reflection opportunities for growth and reflection.

A key benefit of wilderness therapy is its immersive experience. Participants actively engage with nature through activities like hiking, rock climbing, and survival skills training, integral to the therapeutic process. These challenges are physical and metaphorical, representing life's obstacles. Overcoming rugged terrain, for example, fosters a sense of accomplishment and self-efficacy.

Outdoor group therapy sessions enhance their therapeutic impact. Sharing experiences during a hike or around a campfire creates a strong bond among first responders. These shared challenges and triumphs build camaraderie and understanding, surpassing traditional therapy settings. This supportive network acts as a safety net, breaking down emotional barriers and fostering deeper emotional connections.

Wilderness therapy aims to restore first responders' sense of purpose and resilience, with nature as an inspiring backdrop. Through reflection and therapeutic exercises, individuals gain clarity on their purpose, reigniting motivation. Wilderness therapy enables first responders to redefine themselves and find renewed significance in their roles.

Wilderness therapy transcends conventional approaches by integrating nature, physical activities, and group dynamics into an immersive journey of healing, rediscovery, and resilience against life's challenges.

Acupuncture

Acupuncture for first responders is an ancient Chinese therapeutic practice that emphasizes holistic well-being by using needle insertion along meridian pathways of the body to facilitate Qi (vital energy). According to ancient wisdom, disruption of this flow of vital energy leads to physical and psychological symptoms.

Acupuncture is particularly efficient for first responders, who often encounter diverse challenges in their high-stress professions. It has been successful in mitigating the psychological impact of traumatic events, with targeted needle insertion relieving symptoms like anxiety and insomnia. Stimulating specific acupoints helps restore the body's energy equilibrium, fostering a sense of calm and decreasing the heightened arousal often experienced by first responders.

In practice, acupuncture for first responders involves an individualized and comprehensive approach. Trained acupuncturists assess each individual's physical and emotional well being before tailoring a treatment plan specifically to each first responder's needs and experiences. This approach not only alleviates symptoms but also aims to strengthen resilience and overall well-being.

Research indicates that acupuncture can influence various physiological processes, including neurotransmitter release and modulation of the autonomic nervous system. This contributes to regulating stress responses and restoring balance in the body. Furthermore, acupuncture sessions offer first responders a safe space to process emotional experiences, with the therapeutic relationship fostering trust, communication, and emotional healing.

Acupuncture for first responders goes far beyond providing therapeutic relief; it represents an integrative and holistic solution to address their unique challenges. By engaging with the body's energy flow, acupuncture creates balance, alleviates symptoms, and builds resilience in demanding and often traumatic work environments.

Examining alternative therapies for trauma reactions and post-traumatic stress disorder (PTSD) among first responders reveals a wealth of healing modalities beyond conventional approaches. Acknowledging individual variation, tailored and personalized strategies become key in the quest for effective interventions; no single approach fits all, necessitating an exhaustive exploration of different therapeutic techniques.

Eye movement desensitization and reprocessing (EMDR), an emerging alternative therapy, has seen great success among first responders. EMDR utilizes guided lateral eye movements to reprocess distressful memories. Striving to relieve the emotional burden associated with trauma experiences, EMDR encourages adaptive resolution, allowing first responders to gradually confront and reframe memories through systematic desensitization for maximum empowerment and emotional equilibrium.

Mindfulness-based interventions offer another means of alleviating trauma among first responders. Practices such as mindfulness-based stress reduction (MBSR) and mindfulness- based cognitive therapy (MBCT) help individuals cultivate present-moment awareness to reduce intrusive thoughts and memories, thus improving emotional regulation and decreasing symptoms of PTSD.

Equine-assisted therapy provides first responders with an innovative and experiential form of emotional healing through interaction with horses. Horses, being sensitive and intuitive animals, serve as mirrors to our emotions, providing instantaneous feedback while building trust between participants. Equine therapy encourages self-reflection, emotional expression, and the creation of coping mechanisms, offering a nontraditional yet impactful way of managing trauma.

In addition to these specific therapeutic modalities, holistic perspectives on alternative therapies emphasize integrative approaches. Combining techniques like traditional talk therapy with expressive arts therapies like art or music therapy offers comprehensive and tailored healing journeys; yoga and biofeedback practices add another layer to their repertoire for first responders looking for resilience and recovery.

Exploring alternative therapies for trauma reactions and PTSD among first responders requires an ongoing commitment to individual care, considering various approaches that have proven successful over time. Creating a supportive environment that encourages open dialogue between first responders and mental health professionals is essential. By welcoming the wide array of alternative therapies available and personalizing interventions to meet each person's unique needs and preferences, first responders can embark on an extraordinary healing journey, strengthening both their mental wellbeing and their ability to serve their communities effectively.

| 9 |

Chapter 8: Building Resilience and Self-Care Strategies for First Responders

Recognizing the Importance of Self-Care in Mental Health Recovery

First responders face significant mental health challenges that often go overlooked, with resilience and commitment being required from them daily. Recognizing the importance of self- care towards the recovery of mental health cannot be overemphasized.

Self-care should not be seen as just another luxury but as an integral component of overall well-being. This is especially true for first responders, who often deal with trauma reactions and post-traumatic stress disorder (PTSD) as part of their duties.

Mental health therapy for first responders is a specialized field that recognizes their unique challenges in terms of mental health. Instead of simply treating symptoms of trauma, mental health therapy for first responders must incorporate self-care strategies as part of its recovery plan. This acknowledges that self-care is not simply an additional consideration but integral to attaining mental equilibrium.

Police officers, firefighters, paramedics, EMTs, and dispatchers often encounter high-stress and traumatic events that can have a severe negative effect on their psychological well-being. Over time, these experiences often manifest into anxiety, depression, or full-fledged PTSD symptoms. Self-care practices become essential tools in mitigating their lasting effect on mental health.

Self-care should not be approached in an all-or-nothing fashion; customizing strategies according to individual needs and preferences is of the utmost importance. This could involve physical activities, mindfulness practices, and professional counseling - or any combination thereof. Building resilience on an individual and organizational level can significantly assist with mitigating repeated exposure to trauma.

At the core of any comprehensive strategy for strengthening resilience and implementing self- care is a cultural shift within first responder organizations. Encouraging open discussions around mental health issues, normalizing seeking support services, and actively creating an environment that prioritizes the well-being of those who dedicate their lives to public safety is paramount. Integrating mental health awareness programs, peer support networks, and accessible counseling resources all together contribute to creating a more supportive and resilient first responder community.

Understanding and accepting the importance of self-care for first responders navigating the challenging landscape of mental health recovery is of critical importance. By treating it not as a secondary consideration but instead as an indispensable building block, resilience becomes clearer, and mental health equilibrium becomes an inclusive effort that empowers each person to prioritize their well-being. Adopting a comprehensive approach to resilience-building and self-care strategies is of particular importance for first responders who face unique and demanding situations regularly in their duties. Given how these experiences impact mental health, self-care becomes not simply an indulgence but an absolute must.

Building resilience means developing the capacity to overcome difficulties and is closely related to engaging in consistent self-care practices. Engaging in these practices serves as a cornerstone for mental health recovery, helping individuals navigate turbulent professions while mitigating any negative effects on their well-being.

Understanding self-care requires going deeper. While activities like exercise, adequate rest, and nutrition play key roles, true self-care entails taking a holistic approach that addresses emotional, psychological, spiritual, and bodily well-being - this may mean attending regular debriefing sessions with peer support networks as well as accessing mental health resources.

Fostering resilience and self-care for first responders requires an organizational cultural shift. Recognizing and validating the emotional toll of their job is crucial for creating an environment in which seeking help is welcomed rather than stigmatized. Not only does this facilitate mental health recovery, but it also creates a stronger workforce capable of meeting its demands.

As individual preferences and needs can vary considerably, tailoring self-care strategies to align with personal interests, coping mechanisms, strengths, and interests is paramount to their effectiveness. Be it mindfulness practices, artistic outlets, or hobbies; the aim is to facilitate activities that bring genuine joy and relaxation.

Building resilience and implementing self-care strategies for first responders is a complex, multidimensional, and ever-evolving process. Recognizing the connection between self-care and mental health recovery is the initial step, followed by creating an environment that emphasizes well-being. By exploring different aspects of resilience and self-care strategies, we empower first responders not only to withstand but also to flourish in their demanding roles - eventually contributing to a healthier and more resilient community.

Some examples include:

Prioritizing sleep

Prioritizing sleep is particularly important for first responders, who face demanding and unpredictable work schedules that increase their risk of sleep deprivation. Given their critical roles, which require quick decision-making and alertness, ensuring sufficient restorative sleep becomes vitally important. Beyond setting a consistent sleeping schedule, it is necessary to consider the unique obstacles they face in achieving optimal sleep hygiene.

First responders, including paramedics, firefighters, and police officers, often encounter highly stressful and traumatic scenarios during their duties. These emergency responses can produce high levels of physical and psychological arousal, making it challenging for these professionals to unwind and get the restful sleep required for overall well-being. Therefore, any comprehensive plan to prioritize sleep for first responders must incorporate strategies to mitigate occupational stressors that affect their sleep quality.

These professionals face mental and physical demands that can disrupt their sleep, including irregular shift work, extended duty hours, and exposure to environmental factors like noise or bright lights during nighttime operations, which can disrupt circadian rhythms and exacerbate sleep difficulties. Tailored interventions such as strategic shift scheduling, creating conducive sleeping environments at workstations, or providing stress management and coping resources are necessary to protect their restful slumber.

Sleep is a dynamic process crucial for memory consolidation, emotional regulation, and immune function, requiring a nuanced approach when prioritizing it among first responders. Sleep hygiene education, mental health support programs, and accessible resources that assist first responder communities can greatly contribute to creating an atmosphere of well-being in the workforce. By acknowledging the vital role sleep plays in maintaining mental and physical resilience, we empower first responders to fulfill their roles to the fullest while protecting their long-term health and overall quality of life.

Engaging in physical activity

Physical exercise is vital for overall well-being, and for first responders who regularly face intense challenges in their line of duty, it's even more crucial. Engaging in regular physical activity provides more than just stress relief; it plays an instrumental role in mitigating the unique stressors associated with their high-pressure professions. These roles often demand quick decision-making, emotional resilience, and physical endurance, and incorporating regular physical activities into their routine is key to managing these demands and aiding recovery.

One of the primary benefits of regular exercise for first responders is the improvement of cognitive functions. Activities like running, which require sustained cardiovascular effort, increase blood flow to the brain, enhancing cognitive abilities. This is particularly important for handling high-stakes situations where quick thinking and clear-headedness are essential. Yoga, in addition to building physical strength and flexibility, also cultivates mindfulness and stress management techniques, helping first responders remain calm under pressure.

Team sports provide an excellent way for first responders to engage in physical exercise while fostering camaraderie and teamwork. The collaborative nature of these sports directly translates to improved communication and coordination in emergency scenarios. Moreover, the social support gained from participating in team sports combats the potential isolation of their jobs, creating resilient communities of first responders.

Strength training is also crucial for first responders due to the physical demands of their work. Building and maintaining strength is key to preventing injuries. A comprehensive fitness plan that targets various muscle groups helps first responders meet the physical challenges of their duties.

Overall, physical exercise for first responders offers benefits that extend beyond fitness. Tailoring an exercise routine to their specific needs not only boosts physical health but also strengthens their mental capacity to face the demands of their profession. Incorporating activities like running, yoga, team sports, and resistance training contributes to the well-being of first responders, forming an integral part of their wellness approach.

Practicing mindfulness and relaxation techniques:

First responders recognize the immense value of practicing mindfulness and relaxation techniques. Their roles often require confronting high-stress, emotionally charged environments with steadfast dedication. Exploring these techniques reveals more than just temporary respite; they serve as essential tools for cultivating resilience, mental acuity, and overall well-being.

Deep breathing is fundamental in first responder training. Beyond immediate stress relief, deep breathing exercises enhance respiratory function, optimizing oxygen delivery to the brain and body. This leads to improved cognitive performance and focus during critical situations. By practicing deliberate and rhythmic breathing patterns, first responders can manage stress physiologically and foster an environment conducive to sound decision-making amidst chaos.

Meditation is another crucial element for first responders' wellness. Regular meditation sessions help them build mental fortitude and emotional regulation. Through mindfulness meditation, they learn to observe thoughts and emotions without judgment, an invaluable skill when facing difficulties. This greater self-awareness helps guard against burnout, maintaining purposefulness and clarity in their demanding roles.

Mindfulness as an approach extends beyond specific techniques. For first responders, it involves cultivating present-moment awareness in all aspects of life. By focusing on the present, mindfulness helps detach from accumulated stressors, allowing first responders to navigate challenges with composure, reducing risks associated with chronic stress.

Mindfulness and relaxation techniques offer first responders more than conventional stress management. These practices represent a transformative journey towards enhanced mental resilience, emotional well-being, and sustained effectiveness in demanding environments. As they continue to serve and protect, mindfulness practices provide a vital foundation of support, contributing not only to their well-being but also to the effectiveness of emergency response systems.

Seeking social support

Supporting first responders socially is a key component in navigating the challenges of their demanding profession. More than just recognizing its importance, it's essential for first responders to engage deeply with specific forms of support that can significantly impact their mental and emotional well-being amid emergency situations.

One avenue for support is groups specifically designed for the unique experiences of first responders. These groups provide a centralized hub for individuals to share their struggles, triumphs, and insights about their profession, creating a sense of camaraderie among first responders and offering solace in knowing they're not alone in facing its unique challenges.

Colleague interactions play a vital role in providing support networks for first responders. Establishing open channels of communication in the workplace ensures that individuals can express their thoughts and emotions without fear of judgment from coworkers, while regular debriefings and check-ins among colleagues provide valuable opportunities to discuss the emotional toll of experiences and share coping strategies. Fostering team dynamics not only boosts individual resilience but also creates healthier and more cohesive work environments.

Therapy services specializing in therapy for first responders can be particularly valuable. These professionals have an in-depth understanding of the psychological complexities involved with emergency response work and can offer targeted interventions, coping mechanisms, and tailored strategies to help individuals cope with the unique stressors and traumas associated with emergency response work. Therapy also offers first responders a confidential space to explore their emotions freely while building resilience to manage its ongoing effects on their mental well being.

Social support for first responders requires more than just an acknowledgment of its significance; it involves actively engaging with various avenues of assistance, including support groups, building connections with colleagues, and tapping into the expertise of mental health professionals. By adopting this comprehensive approach to obtaining social support, first responders can create resilient networks that not only meet immediate needs but also contribute to the long-term well-being of those devoted to keeping others safe during times of crisis.

Setting boundaries

Setting clear and firm boundaries is vital for first responders' mental and emotional well-being. Their profession often demands them to navigate high-stress situations with limited time for relaxation; therefore, establishing healthy boundaries becomes crucial in maintaining equilibrium for mental and emotional well-being.

First responders such as firefighters, police officers, and emergency medical personnel often find themselves facing challenging circumstances in the line of duty. As individuals dedicated to serving others - often at the risk of neglecting themselves - first responders must recognize and prioritize personal well-being over additional responsibilities and accept them kindly to remain resilient and safe. It becomes an obligation for first responders to learn to say no when additional responsibilities are requested.

Emergency response work can be demanding, and it's crucial that first responders set clear boundaries to avoid burnout. By delineating professional commitments and drawing clear lines between work and personal life, first responders create a barrier against the cumulative stresses inherent in their roles - helping them tackle each task with renewed vigor and resilience.

Setting boundaries doesn't just involve rejecting additional work; it also means acknowledging the significance of self-care. First responders often find themselves immersed in an environment that glorifies sacrifice and resilience over individual needs; however, to ensure a sustainable and resilient workforce, this must change culturally by prioritizing mental, emotional, and physical well-being. This requires encouraging open discussions about the challenges first responders face and creating an atmosphere where seeking support is seen as strength rather than weakness.

Setting boundaries for first responders extends far beyond simply saying no; it requires taking an extensive approach to safeguard their well-being. By cultivating an environment that prioritizes self-care, encourages open dialogue, and makes clear distinctions between professional and personal life, we can contribute to their resilience and longevity - as well as make others safer during moments of crisis.

Building resilience and employing effective self-care strategies are integral parts of first responder wellness, serving as essential building blocks in their mental health recovery journeys. Self-care should not be seen as just an occasional act, but as part of one's ongoing dedication to overall health; prioritizing personal well-being not only promotes individual resilience but is vital in maintaining robust lives within first-response environments.

Self-care is of utmost importance in the demanding environment that first responders work in, serving as an antidote to stress, trauma, and the emotional strain associated with their duties. Recognizing self-care not as an indulgence but as a necessity is key to creating a resilient first responder community.

A deeper investigation of resilience shows a complex process encompassing psychological, emotional, and physical dimensions. Resilience involves not only recovering from hardships but also developing the capacity to adapt and grow under trying circumstances - something first responders often face from critical incidents to the everyday demands of their roles. Cultivating resilience becomes an ongoing journey that changes with each stressor encountered.

One key component of resilience-building for first responders involves cultivating effective coping mechanisms and skills to help navigate stressors more successfully. This includes creating an enabling work environment, accessing mental health resources, and encouraging open dialogue about challenges they are experiencing. Furthermore, resilience building goes beyond individual-level development; it emphasizes creating a sense of community support among first responders as a collective goal.

Recognizing the mutually reinforcing nature of resilience and self-care is central to creating effective strategies tailored specifically to first responders' unique needs. This requires not only responding immediately to stressors but also taking preventive steps and creating long-term support systems. Education and training programs that equip first responders with tools for managing stress can contribute significantly towards building resilient workforces with positive mental health.

First-responder mental health recovery depends heavily on an ongoing commitment to cultivating resilience and practicing effective self-care strategies. By acknowledging the holistic nature of this process and creating an environment that prioritizes well-being, first responders can cultivate the strength needed to endure the pressures associated with their profession while leading fulfilling lives.

Developing Resilience Skills to Cope with Traumatic Experiences

First responders often face emotionally draining situations in their line of duty that can have lasting negative impacts on their mental well-being. Exposure to traumatic events is commonplace in professions like police officers, firefighters, paramedics, EMTs, and 911 dispatchers, making resilience skills crucial for effectively managing these roles. This subchapter provides a comprehensive analysis of strategies and insights aimed at assisting first responders in building resilience against post-traumatic stress disorder (PTSD).

The subchapter delves into the unique challenges faced by different first responder roles, emphasizing the need for tailored approaches to meet their individual needs. It goes beyond acknowledging trauma, focusing on developing resilience in the aftermath of traumatic events.

This includes a nuanced understanding of the psychological impact of such events on first responders and stresses the importance of proactive mental health support. Building resilience is not just a one-time endeavor but requires ongoing nurturing to sustain and build it over time.

At the core of this exploration are coping mechanisms and resilience-building techniques used by first responders. These range from mindfulness practices tailored to the high-stress environments first responders encounter, to targeted psychological interventions aimed at mitigating the negative impacts of trauma. Real-world case studies and success stories are included to highlight the efficacy of these strategies as proactive measures for protecting mental health within first responder communities.

Additionally, the content encourages open dialogue about mental health issues and aims to dispel stigmas that often prevent first responders from seeking help. It explores the use of peer support networks, mental health training programs, and organizational initiatives as ways to encourage and actively nurture resilience. By providing first responders with the necessary tools, the goal is to help them not only survive but also thrive under stressors, building resilient and mentally robust frontline communities.

Understanding Traumatic Reactions and PTSD

Understanding trauma reactions and post-traumatic stress disorders (PTSD) among first responders is essential for a comprehensive approach to mental health in this unique occupational setting. It's important to delve deeper into these responses, recognizing that they are not signs of weakness but natural reactions to extraordinary situations.

First responders frequently face situations that severely test human resilience, subjecting them to extreme stresses with lasting psychological effects. Beyond the immediate impact of distressing incidents, they may experience a range of emotional and psychological challenges over time, including increased anxiety, intrusive memories, emotional numbness, and hypervigilance, which are common signs of trauma. It's crucial to acknowledge first responders' reactions as valid and understandable to address their mental health needs effectively. Understanding that these emotional responses might be adaptive mechanisms to cope with their work can help reduce stigma and create a more supportive environment for seeking help.

Exploring traumatic reactions further highlights the need for individualized and targeted mental health support for first responders. Considering their unique experiences, coping styles, and personal backgrounds, first responders might show varied reactions to trauma. Recognizing this diversity is key to providing more personalized interventions that address the complex nature of trauma in this professional context.

As we delve into this subject, the importance of fostering an open and supportive environment becomes clear. Encouraging open discussions about mental health, ensuring access to resources, and implementing peer support programs are vital steps toward building a more resilient and emotionally healthy first responder community. By gaining a deeper understanding of traumatic reactions and PTSD in first responders, we can develop proactive measures that focus on mental well-being, facilitating healing and recovery.

Building Resilience

First responders often operate under high-stakes conditions that place significant strain and responsibility on them, making resilience not just essential but necessary. Resilience in this context goes beyond merely bouncing back from difficulties; it involves thriving in the face of challenges.

Dealing with traumatizing incidents and intense pressure, first responders require effective strategies to build and sustain resilience. Resilience, while often considered the ability to cope in difficult circumstances, encompasses psychological, emotional, and physical factors.

A key aspect of building resilience within the first responder network is the creation of a supportive community. Fostering open communication and shared experiences allows individuals to express emotions and concerns freely, which can be crucial in relieving stress. Peer support programs provide an invaluable outlet for first responders to process the emotional toll of their work.

Proactive mental health initiatives are integral to resilience-building among first responders. Implementing regular mental health check-ins, counseling services, and resources for psychological well-being helps develop coping mechanisms and stress-management techniques. Training programs are also crucial, offering tools for early identification and treatment of burnout or trauma symptoms to protect long-term mental health.

Physical well-being is closely linked to mental resilience. Fitness and wellness programs tailored to first responder roles are critical. Regular exercise not only maintains physical health but also acts as a stress reliever. Adequate sleep and nutrition are essential, as they directly impact cognitive function and emotional regulation.

Resilience-building strategies should be included in first responder training curriculums. Simulation exercises that mimic real-life challenges give first responders opportunities to test coping mechanisms and build confidence in overcoming adversity.

At its core, building resilience among first responders requires a comprehensive and proactive approach. This includes providing mental health resources, focusing on physical well-being, and incorporating resilience training into professional development. Each component is vital to ensuring the mental resilience of those who dedicate their lives to serving and protecting their communities.

Self-Care for First Responders: Nurturing Well-Being on All Fronts

Prioritizing well-being in the demanding environment of first responders is crucial. It's essential to look beyond traditional physical health measures and understand the interplay of various factors. Engaging in activities that go beyond simple relaxation, like targeted exercises, mindfulness meditation, or personal hobbies, is key to a comprehensive self-care routine. Establishing healthy boundaries transcends mere time management; it's a fundamental practice that secures time for personal activities and nurturing relationships with loved ones. By embracing a broad spectrum of self-care strategies, first responders can fortify themselves against the intense demands of their roles.

Social Support in the First Responder Community: Building Bridges

First responders encounter distinct challenges that require a specialized approach to social support. Connecting with peers who have similar experiences offers a sense of mutual understanding and solidarity. Whether it's through casual chats or formal support groups, sharing feelings and experiences with trusted individuals can offer significant comfort and validation. Therapy from professionals who specialize in mental health for first responders presents a customized solution for navigating the emotional intricacies of their work. Through therapy sessions designed specifically for them, first responders can establish a support network that serves as a bulwark against the potential isolation inherent in their roles.

Stress Management Techniques: Building Resilience into your Toolbox.

Effective stress management is not simply a skill for first responders - it is an indispensable asset in their toolbox. Traditional methods aside, the adoption of advanced stress-relief techniques like deep breathing, progressive muscle relaxation, and cognitive-behavioral therapy (CBT) is vital. These methods, ranging from deep breathing and progressive relaxation to CBT strategies, provide extensive solutions for easing anxiety, managing intrusive thoughts, and enhancing coping skills. By fully embracing a range of techniques, first responders can develop the resilience needed to navigate the unpredictable and high-pressure demands of their work.

Resilient Thinking: Transforming Perspectives to Confront Adversity

Fostering resilience involves more than enduring hardship; it demands a transformative approach to thinking. First responders can nurture a resilient mindset by actively countering negative thoughts and reshaping them positively, embracing setbacks as opportunities for personal growth, and fostering an adaptive growth mindset that perceives challenges as chances for improvement. By examining these principles more deeply, first responders can develop mental strategies that allow them to not just survive but thrive in the face of adversity.

Self-Reflection: Unlocking Emotional Understanding

Self-reflection is more than an empty exercise; it's an introspective exploration of emotions, triggers, and coping mechanisms that lie below the surface. Beyond casual introspection, practices like journaling or engaging in therapeutic dialogue provide structured approaches for processing traumatizing experiences and making sense of them. For first responders, regular self reflection leads to a deeper awareness of their emotional landscape, enhancing their ability to manage the pressures of their work with increased self-awareness and resilience.

Conclusion

Exploring trauma reactions and PTSD among first responders requires a nuanced understanding of their specific challenges. Building resilience becomes not just a recommendation but an integral component in dealing with their often intense and terrifying experiences. This involves more than just conventional coping mechanisms, highlighting the multidimensional nature of resilience.

Central to resilience for first responders is the practice of self-care. It's important to create tailored self-care practices that address not only physical well-being but also mental and emotional health, acknowledging the holistic nature of healing.

Social support is a critical aspect of healing. Recognizing the connection between individual and collective resilience is key in combating the isolating effects of trauma. Encouraging open communication helps first responders draw strength from one another and breaks down stigma associated with seeking help.

Stress management is critical for first responders who often face high-stakes situations. It's important to explore evidence-based techniques specifically designed for their line of duty, focusing on both immediate and long-term strategies to foster sustained well-being.

Resilient thinking is particularly important for first responders, and further investigation into this area is warranted. Understanding the cognitive processes involved in resilient thinking can provide valuable insights into creating environments that promote post-traumatic growth.

Self-reflection is another key aspect that should be emphasized. It allows first responders to process and integrate their emotions, fostering coherence amid trauma. Practices like journaling or debriefing sessions are important for facilitating introspection and are vital for their therapeutic journey.

Recognizing first responders as Unsung Heroes underscores the need for professional mental health therapy services. Overcoming barriers to accessing mental health resources is crucial for beginning a path to healing that honors their resilience and sacrifice. Stress management is critical for first responders who often face high-stakes situations. It's important to explore evidence-based techniques specifically designed for their line of duty, focusing on both immediate and long-term strategies to foster sustained well-being.

Resilient thinking is particularly important for first responders, and further investigation into this area is warranted. Understanding the cognitive processes involved in resilient thinking can provide valuable insights into creating environments that promote post-traumatic growth.

Self-reflection is another key aspect that should be emphasized. It allows first responders to process and integrate their emotions, fostering coherence amid trauma. Practices like journaling or debriefing sessions are important for facilitating introspection and are vital for their therapeutic journey.

Recognizing first responders as unsung heroes underscores the need for professional mental health therapy services. Overcoming barriers to accessing mental health resources is crucial for beginning a path to healing that honors their resilience and sacrifice.

Creating Supportive Work Environments for First Responders

First responders, including firefighters, paramedics, and law enforcement personnel, regularly face a range of challenges and traumatic incidents in their duties. These challenges, spanning physical risks and the profound psychological toll of distressing events, can lead to mental health issues like traumatic reactions and PTSD. Given these serious impacts on mental well-being, comprehensive measures to recognize and actively address these needs are crucial.

Supportive work environments for first responders require an integrated and multifaceted approach, taking into account every aspect of their professional lives. Beyond addressing immediate trauma, long-term mental health care should be integrated into their work environments. This subchapter discusses strategies and initiatives that go beyond acknowledging their struggles, focusing on proactive steps organizations can take to foster environments of psychological resilience, compassion, and understanding.

Key to creating a supportive work environment is implementing tailored training programs. These aim to equip first responders with necessary skills and increase psychological resilience in the face of challenges. Comprehensive mental health training empowers personnel to recognize, cope with, and seek support for the emotional distress caused by their duties, bolstering both individual well-being and community resilience.

Initiatives that demystify mental health support are essential in creating a supportive atmosphere. Offering confidential avenues for first responders to seek counseling services without fear of judgment helps prioritize mental well-being. Additionally, leadership within first responder organizations should foster open dialogue about mental health, emphasizing that seeking help is not a sign of weakness but a necessary step for maintaining longevity in their demanding professions.

An effective work environment for first responders requires ongoing and holistic commitment to their mental well-being, extending beyond the immediate aftermath of traumatic events. By investing in training programs, encouraging open communication, and destigmatizing mental health support, organizations can strengthen their first responder workforces, ensuring they remain capable and effective members of the community.

Tailored Mental Health Resources Available Now

Mental health resources for first responders should be customized to meet their unique needs, avoiding a one-size-fits-all approach. Organizations need to recognize the specific challenges faced by first responders and adapt resources accordingly. This includes providing counseling services specially tailored for first responders, establishing support groups centered around their shared experiences, and setting up hotlines staffed by professionals who understand the nuances of first responder jobs. By tailoring these resources to address the particular concerns and stressors of first responders, organizations can ensure that these needs are met more effectively and appropriately.

Advanced Trauma-Informed Supervision

Supervisors of first responders need to adopt advanced trauma-informed supervision approaches, which require continuous education on mental health and trauma issues. It's crucial that they go beyond just a basic understanding. Supervisors should be adept at recognizing signs of distress in their teams and provide ongoing guidance and support empathetically and compassionately. This approach fosters an environment where first responders feel understood and valued in their workplace. Establishing an accessible leadership structure is key to creating an atmosphere where first responders feel both appreciated and supported. This kind of leadership not only acknowledges their unique challenges but also actively works to provide a supportive and understanding work environment.

Integrative Mental Health Check-ins (IMHCs)

Organizations should go beyond standard mental health check-ins, incorporating assessments into everyday activities, such as post-incident debriefings, and offering confidential options for self-evaluation. By normalizing mental health conversations within the workplace, organizations can more proactively detect and tackle concerns, fostering an environment where seeking help is routinely embraced.

Promoting sustainable work-life balance.

Maintaining a sustainable work-life balance for first responders involves more than just providing time off. It requires fostering a culture that emphasizes the importance of self-care. Organizations should implement policies that not only allow for flexible schedules but also actively support and prioritize self-care activities. This approach is essential in preventing burnout, as it gives first responders the necessary space and time to rejuvenate both physically and mentally. By valuing and encouraging self-care, organizations can help ensure that first responders have the resilience and well-being needed to perform their demanding roles effectively.

Conclusion:

Establishing supportive work environments for first responders is crucial due to the unique demands of their roles. Simply recognizing the mental health challenges they face is not enough; it's important to take proactive steps to create a culture that prioritizes their well-being. Educating organizations about the stressors specific to first responder duties and providing comprehensive training to address potential mental health implications are key, making the process of seeking help more accessible and less stigmatized.

Peer support programs are essential in fostering a strong support network within first responder communities, offering camaraderie and understanding among colleagues with shared experiences. These programs provide a valuable resource for individuals dealing with psychological stress, creating safe spaces for open discussions about mental health concerns.

Organizations should actively invest in mental health resources, ensuring first responders have easy access to counseling, therapy, and other support services. Adopting trauma-informed supervision practices is also important, as it involves training supervisors to understand and address the psychological effects of trauma exposure, thereby creating a more empathetic and supportive work environment.

Promoting work-life balance is crucial for preventing burnout and emotional exhaustion among first responders. Implementing policies that prioritize regular breaks, adequate time off, and flexible schedules can help maintain their mental well-being, job satisfaction, and effectiveness.

Supporting first responders' mental health is vital not only for their individual well-being but also for the effectiveness and compassion of the services they provide to the community. Investing in their mental health creates a more resilient emergency response system.

| 10 |

Chapter 9: Overcoming Barriers to Mental Health Care for First Responders

Addressing Stigma and Cultural Factors in Seeking Mental Health Support

In the first responder community, mental health challenges related to trauma and PTSD often remain hidden, largely due to societal misconceptions and stigma. This exploration aims to address this stigma and identify the cultural factors that make it difficult for first responders to seek support for their mental health needs.

The stigma around mental health is particularly harmful for first responders, who are often expected to maintain strength, resilience, and composure in challenging situations. These expectations can make seeking help difficult, impacting not only their well-being but also their professional standing and career progression. Addressing and dismantling the stigma that marginalizes their vulnerabilities is crucial to recognizing and addressing the genuine struggles they face.

Mental health stigma pervades the first responder community, often seen as contradictory to their perceived image of strength. Cultural biases create obstacles that hinder open discussions about mental well-being, leading to an environment where admitting vulnerability is met with skepticism. Tackling these barriers requires a multifaceted approach that challenges these preconceptions and fosters a culture of empathy, understanding, and proactive support for those struggling with the psychological burdens of their roles.

To provide first responders with the holistic support they deserve, efforts must extend beyond acknowledging mental health challenges to actively dismantling the stigma that often deters them from seeking help. Creating an environment where mental well-being is seen as integral to resilience is essential. Seeking help should be viewed not as a sign of weakness, but as a brave step in managing the emotional demands of the profession. This shift in mindset is crucial in acknowledging that mental health, like physical health, requires care and healing.

Addressing the barriers to mental health care for first responders involves analyzing the individual and collective factors contributing to their reluctance to seek support. The ingrained "tough guy/gal" mentality within the culture can be a significant impediment to acknowledging and addressing mental health issues. This perception often creates a stigmatizing environment around vulnerability, making it even more difficult to seek assistance.

Changing this attitude begins with the understanding that seeking help is a courageous act of self-care. Dismantling the cultural norms that uphold stoicism as a virtue is key. By challenging these norms, we can foster an environment where first responders feel encouraged and supported in seeking mental health therapy and services.

Our examination of strategies and resources for first responders highlights specialized mental health therapy as a crucial element.

Recognizing the unique stressors and challenges faced by this community, therapeutic interventions are tailored to provide support that addresses specific needs like trauma reactions and PTSD.

This discussion also offers guidance on navigating the complexities associated with seeking mental health support. It's important to address concerns about confidentiality and the potential impact on career advancement. Dispelling misconceptions and providing practical solutions empowers first responders to prioritize their mental well-being without fear of repercussions.

Central to our approach is fostering a healing environment within the first responder community. Specifically targeting police officers, 911 dispatchers, firefighters, paramedics, and EMTs, our goal is to encourage these professionals to prioritize their mental health. By creating an environment that acknowledges and values mental well-being, we aim to provide the necessary support. This effort contributes to a paradigm shift that recognizes and actively supports the mental health needs of those on the front lines.

Improving Access to Mental Health Services for First Responders

Introduction

First responders, such as police officers, 911 dispatchers, firefighters, paramedics, and EMTs, are often on the frontlines of crises, facing stressors and trauma events unique to their demanding occupations. These experiences increase their risk for mental health challenges, including trauma reactions and post-traumatic stress disorder (PTSD), which can have lasting effects on these dedicated professionals.

Recognizing the toll their profession takes on mental resilience is crucial, and this subchapter focuses on strategies to increase access to mental health services tailored specifically for first responders.

Considering their commitment to public safety, it's important to understand the specific challenges they face and develop approaches that proactively address all aspects of their mental health.

One key component of providing adequate mental health support is designing specific programs for first responders. These should include counseling, therapy, and psychoeducation, offered by professionals well-versed in trauma response. Additionally, creating a stigma-free environment around mental health in first responder communities is vital. Initiatives promoting open dialogue about seeking mental health support as a positive step for well-being, rather than a weakness, are essential in supporting first responders.

Proactive integration of mental health resources into the workflow of first responders is crucial. This can include incorporating mental health check-ins into professional development training, offering ongoing stress management techniques, and providing access to confidential mental health support services. Integrating mental health considerations into their daily routines acts as a preventative measure, potentially reducing the long-term effects of trauma exposure.

Collaboration between mental health professionals, first responder agencies, and relevant governmental bodies is key to the success of mental health initiatives. Establishing partnerships that aid in creating and implementing effective mental health programs can build a comprehensive support system. Additionally, advocating for policy changes that prioritize mental health in first responder communities, including securing adequate funding, is essential for sustainably addressing their unique challenges.

To effectively improve access to mental health services for first responders, a broad and multifaceted strategy is needed. This strategy should encompass tailored programs, cultural shifts, integration into daily activities, collaborative efforts across various sectors, and a thorough understanding of their experiences and challenges. Such an approach will enable society to better recognize and support these unsung heroes who commit themselves to public safety, often without seeking recognition in return.

Increasing Awareness and Education

Awareness and education about mental health services are vital for building a culture of well- being in the first responder community. It's important to not only recognize symptoms but also to delve into various mental health conditions common among first responders, such as PTSD, depression, anxiety, and other unique psychological challenges specific to their profession.

Efforts to eliminate the stigma associated with seeking help must extend beyond a basic understanding of mental health. Workshops and training sessions should include real-life situations to provide first responders with a detailed knowledge of the challenges they and their peers might face. Additionally, these educational initiatives should be more than traditional classroom settings, using immersive and interactive methods for greater impact.

Mandatory mental health education programs tailored for first responder communities are essential. These programs should specifically address the unique stresses and triggers inherent in their roles, with content tailored for police officers, firefighters, EMTs, and other first responders. By designing an in-depth curriculum tailored specifically towards first responders' experiences we can create an educational framework that is both relevant and impactful.

Creating an environment that encourages open dialogue is key to increasing awareness about mental health among first responders. Implementing peer support programs, mentorship initiatives, and appointing mental health advocates within the first responder community are crucial steps in normalizing conversations about mental well-being.

To effectively elevate awareness and education about mental health services for first responders, a holistic and integrative approach is needed. This involves understanding the specific challenges faced in their professions, employing engaging and interactive educational methods, and fostering open communication within first responder communities. Through these efforts, we can help establish a supportive and resilient mental health culture among first responders.

Implementing Peer Support Programs

Comprehensive peer support programs such as critical incident stress management (CISM), critical incident response (CIR), and peer mentoring are essential for meeting the unique mental health needs of first responders. These initiatives go beyond providing a platform for sharing experiences; rather, they offer structured frameworks designed to ensure the mental well- being of those frequently facing high-stress situations.

CISM is a crucial element of peer support, offering a systematic ap-proach to dealing with the psychological aftermath of critical incidents. It provides debriefing sessions, group discussions, and individual coun-seling by trained peers, helping first responders manage the emotional impacts of traumatic experiences and reducing potential long-term trauma effects.

CIR complements CISM by taking proactive steps to prevent and manage stress. It includes training sessions, resilience-building activities, and creating coping mechanisms, all designed to help first responders develop resilient mindsets and access tools to navigate their demanding roles more effectively. This approach equips first responders to cope better with stressors, aiming to decrease the long-term mental health concerns associated with their profession.

Peer mentoring adds another layer of support for first responders, pairing experienced personnel with less experienced colleagues. This approach promotes camaraderie and trust, providing a safe space for discussing challenges, sharing guidance and coping strategies, and offering emotional support. It's not just about practical knowledge transfer; it's also about fostering emotional support within peer groups.

Integrating programs like CISM, CIR, and Peer Mentoring into workplace culture is crucial and requires leadership commitment, training in peer support, and efforts to destigmatize discussions about mental health. By creating an environment where open conversations about mental health issues are welcomed, first responders can feel more comfortable acknowledging their struggles and seeking professional assistance.

Implementing comprehensive peer support programs such as CISM, CIR, and Peer Mentoring is a multifaceted approach to addressing the mental health needs of first responders. These initiatives do more than just offer platforms for sharing experiences; they provide structured support, resilience-building strategies, and ongoing mentorship to build a culture that prioritizes the well-being of those in public service.

Collaborating with Mental Health Professionals

Nurturing strong relationships between first responder agencies and mental health professionals is key to ensuring the well-being of those in high-stress roles. An approach that extends beyond traditional mental health services is needed, given the unique challenges first responders face. Such collaboration allows for a deeper understanding of the specific stressors and trauma they experience, leading to the development of more targeted interventions.

Collaboration between mental health experts and first responder organizations is essential for crafting specialized treatment programs. These should address both the immediate and long- term mental health needs of first responders. Routine assessments could incorporate mental health screenings as early detection mechanisms for potential issues; this proactive approach helps prevent the escalation of concerns while encouraging resilience within first responder communities and creating a culture of psychological well-being among them.

On-site therapy services at first responder facilities could also be a component of this collaboration. Providing accessible and confidential spaces for therapy addresses the stigma around mental health support and accommodates the demanding schedules of first responders, encouraging a proactive approach to mental well-being.

Developing an efficient referral process that connects first responders with therapists specializing in trauma and PTSD is a vital component of the collaboration between first responder agencies and mental health professionals. Given the specific nature of traumas encountered by first responders, these referrals should ensure access to care that is specifically tailored to their unique experiences. This approach not only increases the effectiveness of treatments but also highlights the importance of seeking help from mental health specialists who understand the first responder profession.

The collaboration between first responder agencies and mental health professionals is more than just coordination; it's a comprehensive effort to meet the mental health needs of those dedicated to public safety. This partnership, encompassing strategic planning, proactive interventions, and a focus on specialist care, demonstrates a deep commitment to the psychological well-being of first responders. It's an essential step in ensuring that those who protect and serve the community have access to the mental health support they need.

Creating Flexible and Confidential Services

Enhancing access to mental health services for first responders calls for innovative and adaptable solutions that align with their demanding schedules and unique challenges. A multifaceted approach is essential, involving tailored services that consider time-sensitive needs and incorporate technological advancements and outreach strategies.

One way to achieve flexibility is by providing mental health services outside of traditional hours. Offering evening or weekend therapy sessions can be a significant boon for first responders who work unpredictable hours. This approach ensures that support is accessible when it's most convenient, guaranteeing that help is available whenever needed.

The adoption of technological innovations is also crucial in making mental health services more accessible to first responders. Online counseling platforms allow them to attend sessions from their homes or any location that suits them, removing the barriers of physical distance. This method offers the necessary support with the convenience and discretion that online platforms provide.

Mobile mental health units are a novel solution for bringing mental health services directly to first responders in their work environments or local areas. These units provide a discreet setting for consultations, offering a non-intimidating and accessible option for those who might be hesitant to use traditional channels. By delivering services right to their doorstep, mobile units significantly reduce transport and scheduling challenges, leading to more personalized care.

In creating an environment where first responders feel comfortable seeking mental health support, flexibility and confidentiality are key. Implementing strict privacy measures and emphasizing confidentiality in counseling sessions are crucial. Protecting sensitive information and building trust between mental health professionals and first responders encourages open communication and allows for a deeper exploration of their challenges, leading to more effective therapeutic relationships.

Establishing flexible and confidential mental health services for first responders involves an adaptable and comprehensive strategy. This includes unconventional scheduling practices, leveraging technological innovations, and utilizing unique outreach strategies. Transforming the mental health landscape for first responders means removing barriers to access, building trust within the profession, and providing specialized support tailored to their specific needs and challenges.

Conclusion

Addressing the mental health needs of first responders facing trauma and PTSD is a pressing, multifaceted challenge. Recognizing the profound impact that exposure to traumatic events has on their well-being is crucial. Beyond acknowledgment, understanding the complexities of these experiences is key to mitigating their psychological effects.

Intensifying awareness campaigns to destigmatize mental health issues within the first responder community is an important part of this approach. Creating an environment where seeking help is seen as a strength, not a weakness, can help shift the culture towards proactive mental well-being. Public education initiatives are essential in dispelling mental illness myths and fostering empathy and understanding among peers, families, and the broader community.

Similarly, developing and implementing comprehensive peer support programs is vital in addressing the issue of burnout among first responders. Programs that provide a space for open and confidential conversation, facilitated by peers who understand the unique job-related stressors, can offer significant support. Such safe spaces allow first responders to share their struggles without fear of judgment, offering them the understanding and support they need from those who can relate to their experiences.

Establishing collaborative partnerships between first responder organizations and mental health professionals is essential. Integrating mental health expertise directly into first responder teams allows for proactive mental health assessments, early intervention, and the development of training programs tailored to their specific challenges.

To serve first responders' complex mental health needs effectively, services must be accessible, flexible, and confidential. This involves adapting support to fit their demanding schedules and unpredictable work environments. Implementing solutions like virtual counseling services, mobile crisis intervention units, and 24/7 helplines can provide timely and crucial assistance.

An integrative approach is needed to improve access to mental health services for first responders experiencing trauma and PTSD. This includes fostering an understanding environment, establishing peer support programs, engaging in collaborative efforts with mental health professionals, and designing services specifically for first responders. Such measures can dismantle barriers and ensure these community heroes receive the support they need to not only endure but also excel in their demanding roles.

Prioritizing mental health for first responders is not just a moral imperative but also a critical investment in their continued ability to serve and protect with resilience and strength.

Collaborating with the Community to Support First Responders' Mental Health

First responders encounter numerous challenges in their daily work that can lead to trauma reactions and post-traumatic stress disorder (PTSD). These mental health issues not only affect their well-being but can also impact their ability to provide effective, compassionate care. Addressing these challenges requires a comprehensive approach, emphasizing collaboration between first responders and their communities.

Community engagement is vital in offering mental health therapy to first responders dealing with trauma and PTSD. Interaction with organizations, mental health professionals, residents, and peer support programs, or even sharing experiences, are crucial for first responders seeking understanding and support. Peer support programs, where experienced first responders provide guidance, empathy, and resources, are particularly beneficial.

Organizing events and workshops by community organizations can increase public awareness of the unique mental health challenges faced by first responders. These initiatives can foster deeper empathy for their struggles, reduce stigmatization, and create a supportive atmosphere where first responders feel encouraged to seek help.

Mental health professionals with expertise in treating first responders are invaluable, as they understand the specific symptoms and challenges faced by police officers, firefighters, paramedics, and dispatchers. Establishing connections with these specialized therapists allows first responders to access personalized therapy tailored to their distinct needs.

Family involvement in the healing process of first responders is also crucial. Families directly observe the impact of traumatic experiences on their loved ones, making their support and understanding critical. Community organizations can provide resources, support groups, and educational programs to help families cope with their emotional challenges and learn how to effectively support their first-responder family members.

Collaboration between community members and first responders is key to providing the emotional support necessary for healing, particularly for those dealing with trauma reactions and PTSD. Integrating peer support programs, awareness initiatives, collaboration with specialized mental health professionals, and family engagement can create an optimal environment for healing. This approach not only reduces stigma but also ensures that our dedicated first responders receive the comprehensive care and assistance they deserve.

| 11 |

Chapter 10: Case Studies and Success Stories

Real-Life Examples of First Responders Overcoming Traumatic Reactions and PTSD

Delve into the world of real-life case studies and success stories to witness the remarkable resilience of first responders as they navigate through the challenges of trauma reactions and post-traumatic stress disorder (PTSD). These stories shed light on the multifaceted nature of trauma and the effectiveness of mental health interventions tailored for first responders.

In one moving case, a veteran police officer, haunted by distressing experiences on duty, battled nightmares, anxiety, and hypervigilance. Seeking solace, the officer turned to specialized therapy designed for law enforcement, like cognitive-behavioral therapy (CBT) and exposure therapy. These methods provided a pathway to gradual healing, reinstating a sense of normalcy and underscoring the critical need for therapies specifically crafted for first responders.

Another poignant example is that of a 911 dispatcher, weighed down by the emotional burden of constantly handling distressing calls, spiraling towards PTSD. Finding comfort in a support group specifically for dispatchers, this individual discovered a community of peers with shared experiences. Engaging in this supportive environment, where coping mechanisms and strategies were exchanged, significantly aided their journey to recovery.

Firefighters, often encountering horrific incidents involving both human and natural disasters, tread a difficult path of psychological recovery. One firefighter's journey in overcoming posttraumatic stress disorder (PTSD) included participating in a comprehensive mental health program. This program, incorporating psychoeducation, mindfulness practices, peer support, and holistic approaches like yoga, proved pivotal not only for managing immediate symptoms but also in building long-term resilience within their firefighting community.

Paramedics and Emergency Medical Technicians (EMTs) face similar challenges due to trauma exposure. A notable case study involves an EMT who, after experiencing vicarious trauma firsthand, took proactive steps towards mental health recovery. Through debriefing sessions, individual therapy, and resilience training, the EMT not only successfully managed the impact on herself but also became an advocate for mental health awareness within the EMS community. By taking such proactive measures, the EMT also mitigated future effects, setting a precedent in her community.

These stories highlight the transformative power of targeted mental health interventions for first responders. By examining these cases, we gain insight into the various strategies effective in treating trauma and PTSD, offering hope and guidance for recovery and resilience in a profession deeply affected by psychological trauma.

Officer Smith's Journey:

Officer Smith, an outstanding member of the law enforcement community, found himself grappling with the emotional aftermath of a profoundly distressing event, which led to haunting nightmares, persistent anxiety, and overwhelming emotional turmoil. Determined to overcome these daunting challenges and heal, Officer Smith embarked on a brave journey towards resilience, aiming to emerge stronger and healed.

Recognizing the severity of his emotional upheaval, Officer Smith proactively sought regular targeted mental health therapy. These sessions offered a sanctuary where he could openly confront and process the intense emotions tied to his traumatic experience. Guided by experienced mental health professionals, he delved into the depths of his psychological distress, unraveling the complex web of thoughts and emotions that had entangled him.

In his quest for healing, Officer Smith discovered and embraced various coping strategies that transcended mere survival, becoming vital tools for regaining his mental equilibrium. Deep breathing exercises emerged as a cornerstone of his recovery, helping to anchor him and alleviate feelings of panic or anxiety. Grounding techniques also became crucial, enabling him to manage intrusive memories without being overwhelmed by them.

As Officer Smith engaged with his therapeutic interventions, the impact was profound and swift: the nightmares that once plagued his nights began to fade, replaced by a newfound sense of calm and resilience; the grip of persistent anxiety loosened, allowing for a growing sense of confidence; and the emotional distress that had once seemed insurmountable gradually transformed into increasing inner strength.

Officer Smith's journey of trauma recovery resonated beyond his own experience. His commitment and resilience became a beacon of inspiration for his fellow officers who were silently facing similar challenges. By openly sharing his journey and the effective strategies that helped him reclaim his life, Officer Smith not only broke down the stigma surrounding mental health in law enforcement but also ignited hope and motivation among other officers grappling with similar issues.

His triumph over the debilitating effects of trauma not only marked a personal victory but also served as a powerful testament to the importance of prioritizing mental health in high-stress professions like law enforcement. Officer Smith's story stands as a compelling example of resilience, the efficacy of therapy, and the commitment required to overcome traumatic experiences. It demonstrates that with adequate support and determination, individuals can not only recover from post-traumatic stress but also drive positive change within their communities.

Dispatcher Martinez's Recovery

Dispatcher Martinez's experience as a 911 operator took a significant turn when an emotionally charged call not only caused immediate stress but also triggered flashbacks and panic attacks, highlighting the intense mental impact on frontline responders. This moment led her to acknowledge the necessity of professional help.

Seeking the expertise of a trauma therapist, Dispatcher Martinez embarked on a journey of intensive, personalized treatment to heal the deep emotional wounds inflicted by her experiences. Her therapy included evidence-based approaches like cognitive-behavioral therapy (CBT) and eye movement desensitization and reprocessing therapy (EMDR), aimed at confronting and processing the trauma-inducing memories deeply embedded in her psyche.

CBT, renowned for its effectiveness, helped Dispatcher Martinez to dissect and alter her negative thought patterns related to her trauma. In structured sessions, she learned to identify and counteract distorted beliefs, replacing them with healthier cognitive patterns. This process not only provided her with coping mechanisms but also built resilience, enabling her to navigate the challenges of her profession with new-found strength and clarity.

Dispatcher Martinez's treatment included eye movement desensitization and reprocessing (EMDR), an innovative therapy a therapy specifically designed to alleviate the emotional distress linked to traumatic memories. In this innovative approach, her therapist guided her through bilateral stimulation exercises, often involving rapid eye movements, to process these traumatic experiences more effectively and reduce their emotional impact.

Her commitment to her mental health and the therapeutic process played a critical role in her recovery. Through active engagement in these evidence-based therapies, Dispatcher Martinez not only addressed the immediate symptoms of PTSD but also cultivated a resilient mindset. This resilience was crucial in helping her successfully manage the demands of her challenging profession.

Dispatcher Martinez's story underscores the importance of recognizing and addressing the mental health needs of first responders. It highlights the need to create a supportive environment that prioritizes their well-being and acknowledges the role of evidence-based interventions as critical tools in facilitating healing and recovery. This real-life example serves as a testament to the power of dedicated mental health care in transforming the lives of those who serve on the front lines.

Firefighter Brown's Triumph:

Firefighter Brown's experience with trauma reactions and PTSD is a powerful example of the resilience and strength first responders exhibit in the face of adversity. Following a perilous situation during a fire rescue operation, Brown was deeply affected emotionally, to the point where he could no longer pursue the firefighting career he was once passionate about. The trauma he experienced cast a shadow over his well-being, marking a significant turning point in his life.

In his quest for healing, Brown turned to a mental health therapist specializing in treating firefighters, embarking on a path to recovery through prolonged exposure therapy (PET). This therapy method carefully exposed him to the memories and emotions associated with the traumatic event, aiding him in processing the distress and breaking down the barriers created by PTSD, ultimately helping him regain control over his mental health.

Returning to firefighting was a challenging process, testing the resilience he had built. With the support of his therapist, colleagues, and a tailored rehabilitation plan, Brown not only resumed his firefighting career but also thrived. His story is a compelling reminder of how individuals can transform trauma into an opportunity for personal growth, emerging not just as survivors but as individuals who have harnessed their experiences for positive change.

Firefighter Brown's contributions following his recovery extend well beyond his personal achievements. His commitment to mentoring others who face similar mental health challenges demonstrates his compassion and significant impact. By sharing his experiences and insights, he has become a source of comfort and guidance for first responders dealing with trauma. Brown's actions have not only inspired others but also fostered a supportive community within the firefighting profession, helping to dismantle the stigma surrounding discussions of mental health.

His story embodies the profound change that is possible when individuals confront and overcome trauma and PTSD. Brown's journey underscores the effectiveness of therapeutic interventions and the crucial role of community support and mentoring in the healing process. He stands as a beacon of hope, encouraging others to seek the help they need, commit to their recovery, and emerge stronger from their experiences. Firefighter Brown's example inspires others to face their challenges, seek assistance, and ultimately grow stronger through their journey to recovery.

Paramedic Johnson's Road to Recovery

Paramedic Johnson's experience powerfully demonstrates the impact of repeated trauma exposure on first responder mental health. Facing daily emergency scenarios, she struggled with severe anxiety and nightmares, a testament to the psychological toll such experiences can take and the necessity for robust mental health support in first responder communities.

Taking proactive steps towards regaining mental balance, Paramedic Johnson sought help from a therapist specializing in trauma. This move was a turning point in her recovery journey, as she engaged in a therapy program that combined individual and group sessions. This approach was instrumental in uncovering layers of emotional distress and providing insight into her behavioral triggers.

The therapy process proved invaluable for Johnson. It not only helped her identify triggers but also equipped her with effective coping mechanisms and emotional regulation tools. These skills were essential in navigating her mental complexities with resilience and strength.

Additionally, she recognized the importance of self-care practices, ensuring a balance between the demands of her job and her mental health. Johnson's story underscores the importance of mental health support for first responders and the effectiveness of personalized therapeutic interventions.

Paramedic Johnson's journey underscores the critical role of a strong support network in trauma recovery. Group therapy offered her a platform to connect with peers facing similar challenges, helping to alleviate the isolation often associated with trauma. This environment validated her experiences and reinforced the idea that seeking help is an act of courage, not weakness.

As she navigated her way through the aftermath of her trauma, Johnson's path to healing became a powerful testament to human resilience. Returning to her role in emergency response, now equipped with a robust set of coping strategies and a stronger foundation in mental health, she exemplified the positive impact of proactive mental health care for emergency responders. Johnson's story highlights the importance of prioritizing and normalizing mental wellness in first-response communities, contributing to the development of healthier, more supportive emergency response environments.

Conclusion

Real-life stories vividly illustrate the significant impact mental health therapy can have on first responders grappling with trauma reactions and post-traumatic stress disorder (PTSD). These individuals, who routinely encounter high-stress scenarios and witness harrowing events, often bear a heavy psychological burden. Yet, the narratives of those who have successfully journeyed through recovery shine as beacons of hope, demonstrating the effectiveness of evidence-based treatments in facilitating healing.

Take, for instance, a paramedic who, after years in emergency response, began to suffer from intrusive memories and nightmares of past traumatic incidents. Realizing the need for intervention, they turned to cognitive-behavior therapy (CBT), a method known for its efficacy in treating PTSD. Through specialized sessions, they learned to reshape negative thought patterns and developed strategies to manage the impact of intense calls. This journey not only helped lessen their trauma but also restored a sense of control over their mental health.

Another powerful example is found in eye movement desensitization and reprocessing (EMDR) therapy. A seasoned firefighter, haunted by a particularly perilous rescue, sought EMDR treatment from a therapist experienced in this field. This innovative therapy, which includes techniques like guided eye movements to process distressing memories, led to a marked decrease in the emotional intensity linked to the traumatic event, further validating the effectiveness of such tailored therapeutic approaches.

Psychodramatic Experiential Therapy (PET) was instrumental for a police officer grappling with the aftermath of a life-threatening situation. Conducted by a skilled therapist, PET used role-playing exercises to recreate and process challenging incidents. This approach facilitated emotional expression and camaraderie among first responders, addressing individual trauma while simultaneously building resilience and understanding within their community.

Group therapy, a vital component of recovery for many first responders, was particularly beneficial for an EMT facing job-related stress. Joining a support group specifically for emergency medical technicians allowed this individual to share experiences with colleagues who understood their unique challenges. This experience provided not only validation but also a sense of companionship, highlighting the importance of seeking help within one's professional community.

By highlighting these examples, we emphasize the transformative impact of mental health therapy for first responders overcoming trauma and PTSD. Adopting evidence-based treatments and fostering supportive communities enables these professionals to not only recover their mental well-being but also to demonstrate resilience and strength within the first responder community. Their stories are powerful endorsements of the value of seeking help and prioritizing mental health on the journey to healing.

Insights from Experts and Clinicians in the Field

Experts and clinicians specializing in mental health therapy for first responders with trauma and PTSD provide valuable insights into the challenges faced by emergency service professionals. These professionals, including psychologists and trauma specialists, offer a depth of understanding that extends beyond traditional therapy approaches. They provide a holistic perspective on the mental well-being of police officers, 911 dispatchers, firefighters, paramedics, and EMTs.

Applying their extensive experience in working with first responders, these specialists deliver mental health solutions specifically tailored to the unique requirements of different emergency service roles. Their approach encompasses not only extensive knowledge but also deep empathy for the specific circumstances and pressures inherent to first responder careers. This combination of compassion and understanding enables them to effectively address trauma, offering therapies that are specifically designed for the unique needs of this professional community.

As these experts unravel the complex mechanisms causing trauma-induced mental health disorders and posttraumatic stress reactions (PTSD), their expertise brings trauma's devastating impact into sharp focus. By investigating triggers and symptoms common among various first responder roles, practitioners and individuals gain an unparalleled insight into the psychological toll imposed by such professions This leads to the creation of tailored therapeutic interventions that are specifically geared to meet the individual challenges associated with service in emergency response roles.

Acknowledging the different experiences of police officers, paramedics, firefighters, and other first responders, these mental health professionals emphasize the importance of an individualized and adaptable approach to therapy. They recognize that the stressors and traumas unique to each role require specific treatment strategies, advocating for a therapeutic landscape that is empathetic and responsive to the diverse experiences of first responders.

Police Officers

Experts and clinicians specializing in mental health therapy for first responders provide critical insights that extend beyond simple observations. Their commitment to understanding and addressing the long-term impacts of trauma is invaluable for those in high-risk professions like law enforcement, firefighting, and emergency medical services. Their expertise is essential in creating compassionate, effective support systems specifically designed for the unique challenges faced by first responders.

These professionals shed light on the specific ways in which police officers, for instance, might experience trauma reactions and post-traumatic stress disorder (PTSD). Their insights emphasize the importance of considering the long-term effects of repeated exposure to violence, danger, and high-stress situations. This understanding highlights the complexity of challenges faced by law enforcement personnel and the need for multifaceted strategies to maintain their mental health.

Furthermore, these experts delve into the factors that contribute to the psychological strain of police officers. They examine how ongoing exposure to traumatic events can gradually erode resilience, and emphasize the importance of proactive steps to reinforce mental well-being. Their insights also extend to the internal psychological dynamics affecting officers' cognitive and emotional responses, ensuring a comprehensive approach to understanding and managing the mental health challenges unique to first responders.

Experts in the field of mental health for law enforcement professionals offer specialized strategies tailored to the complex nature of trauma faced by police officers. These strategies focus on strengthening resilience and enhancing coping mechanisms, going beyond conventional therapeutic approaches. They take into account the unique challenges police officers face on duty and adapt interventions to each officer's individual experiences and the specific stressors they encounter in their work.

The recommendation of evidence-based therapies by these experts and clinicians is crucial in promoting mental well-being among police officers. It's important that these therapeutic modalities are not only tailored to fit the law enforcement context but also grounded in empirical research. Professionals in this field aim to provide targeted and effective interventions that encompass the various types of trauma experienced by officers.

In addressing trauma reactions and PTSD in police officers, these experts and clinicians delve into the deeper layers of psychological, emotional, and occupational challenges specific to law enforcement. Their commitment to employing strategies and evidence-based therapies is a testament to their dedication to meeting the individual needs of this population. Recognizing and fostering resilience is seen as key to success in the often challenging profession of law enforcement.

Firefighters

Experts and clinicians provide valuable insights into the complex mental health landscape of firefighters. They shed light on the deep psychological impacts that come from regularly witnessing life-threatening situations, leaving emotional scars that extend far beyond the fire scenes.

Clinicians often emphasize the prevalence of survivor's guilt among firefighters, which can profoundly affect their psyche following critical incidents. The tendency to dwell on what might have been done differently during traumatic events can lead to lasting emotional scars. It's crucial to understand and address these feelings to foster mental resilience, helping firefighters balance their duties with their inherent humanity.

The impact of traumatic experiences often transcends the boundaries of the fireground, affecting personal relationships and straining familial and social connections in ways that might not be immediately apparent. Clinicians explore the intricate relationship between the demands of firefighting and its effects on family and social ties. Experts provide essential insights into recognizing and addressing these challenges, developing strategies that aid firefighters in managing their well-being and fortifying their interpersonal relationships.

In response to these unique challenges, clinicians offer tailored therapeutic interventions specifically designed for firefighters. Utilizing evidence-based approaches and specialized counseling techniques, their aim is to provide coping mechanisms that surpass typical mental health support services. This holistic approach addresses immediate symptoms while building resilience, enabling firefighters to withstand the trials inherent in their profession.

Expert and clinician insights together paint a comprehensive picture of the psychological challenges faced by firefighters. Acknowledging their experiences and proposing in-depth therapeutic interventions, including trauma management, resilience training, and fostering strong human connections, these professionals offer a detailed and insightful overview of the support needed to aid these dedicated individuals in their careers and lives.

Paramedics and EMTs

In emergency medical services, our expert clinicians adopt a comprehensive approach to understanding the challenges faced by paramedics and EMTs. Their expertise extends to analyzing the emotional impact of providing care in high-pressure situations. They delve into the depths of the experiences of these frontline healthcare providers, uncovering layers of trauma reactions, including post-traumatic stress disorder (PTSD), that go beyond the superficial.

These experts, with their profound knowledge of psychological intricacies, address issues like compassion fatigue and burnout, which are prevalent in the emergency medical field. They provide a range of tools, strategies, and coping mechanisms tailored to meet the unique requirements of emergency medical professionals, going beyond standard coping techniques.

As these experts examine self-care and psychological well-being for paramedics and EMTs, they emphasize its importance both for individuals and within the emergency medical services system. They develop personalized strategies to tackle specific challenges encountered in their line of work, such as fostering a supportive environment among EMS teams and advocating for comprehensive mental health resources. Their aim is to shift the paradigm in how the emotional aspects of emergency medical care are perceived and managed.

Their insights and analysis delve deeply into the trauma and stress that paramedics and EMTs experience, offering a thorough examination of the profession. This exploration is not only about overcoming but also thriving amidst the challenges of trauma reactions and post-traumatic stress disorder (PTSD).

911 Dispatchers

Recognizing the critical role that 911 dispatchers play in emergency response systems, our experienced clinicians have conducted a comprehensive examination of their unique challenges. This goes beyond acknowledging the difficult responsibilities they face; dispatchers often experience trauma vicariously through phone calls. Our investigation delves into the details of the emotional toll incurred from such experiences.

Our exploration into the world of 911 dispatching involves a meticulous analysis of its complex dimensions. We are particularly focused on understanding the long-term effects on dispatchers' mental health. By examining the relationship between handling emergency calls, their psychological aftereffects, and the physical exhaustion that comes with being frontline responders, our experts aim to gain deeper insight into the emotional terrain navigated by 911 dispatchers.

Our study extends beyond merely recognizing the challenges faced by 911 dispatchers. We aim to provide insightful recommendations and practical guidance for managing traumatic reactions and PTSD in this profession. Recognizing the need for tailored therapeutic approaches for individual dispatchers, our clinicians suggest specific strategies to help reduce their psychological toll.

By drawing on empirical research and the experiences of experts who have worked closely with 911 dispatchers, we aim to offer a fuller picture of the emotional challenges inherent in this vital profession. Our exploration into trauma and PTSD in the context of emergency dispatch seeks not only to shed light on often overlooked aspects of this role but also to contribute to the broader conversation on mental health support for these unsung heroes of the emergency response system.

Veteran experts and clinicians in the field of first responder mental health offer invaluable insights for addressing the challenges faced by those enduring trauma reactions or post- traumatic stress disorder (PTSD). Their collective wisdom provides a crucial guide, featuring therapeutic interventions specifically tailored to the unique experiences of these brave individuals.

These experts stress the importance of acknowledging and understanding traumatic reactions in first responders. By gaining insight into PTSD triggers and symptoms, first responders can navigate their recovery with increased self-awareness and efficacy. This understanding enables them to more effectively tackle the significant impacts of their experiences.

Expert and clinical perspectives illuminate the range of therapeutic approaches beneficial for first responders working through trauma and PTSD. These include evidence-based treatments like cognitive-behavioral therapy (CBT) and innovative techniques such as eye movement desensitization and reprocessing (EMDR). Covering all available interventions extensively allows first responders to make well-informed decisions about their mental health treatment, ensuring it aligns with their specific needs and preferences.

Beyond offering therapeutic pathways, these insights create a compassionate and supportive environment for first responders. Experts and clinicians provide tailored advice for developing resilience, coping strategies, and sustainable self-care practices. This comprehensive approach integrates physical, emotional, psychological, and self-care wellness, offering holistic and lasting solutions for those at the forefront of crisis response.

The guidance from experts and clinicians serves as a beacon for first responders, leading them towards a deeper understanding of their trauma and PTSD. Applying this expert knowledge in their recovery journey enables these heroes to find relief and healing that not only restores their well-being but also honors the resilience and dedication they exhibit in high-pressure situations.

| 12 |

Conclusion: A Call to Action for First Responders' Mental Health

Recognizing the Importance of Mental Health Care for First Responders

Exploring the intricate landscape of mental health care for first responders reveals a profound necessity to recognize and prioritize their well-being. These extraordinary individuals dedicate their lives to protecting and serving our communities, dedicated to protecting and serving communities, confront not only the apparent psychological effects of their roles but also more subtle, often hidden burdens.

Essential to this mission is the recognition and treatment of post-traumatic stress disorder (PTSD) among first responders. Their high-stakes work environments and intense experiences can lead to significant, lasting psychological effects. Mental health care for this group must carefully consider both the physical demands and the emotional and psychological burdens unique to their profession.

The discourse on mental health therapy for first responders highlights its crucial role. It involves understanding the various stressors and traumas they regularly face and developing interventions tailored to their unique situations. There's a strong emphasis on the importance of seeking professional help, not as a sign of weakness but as a necessary step for maintaining resilience and enduring the demands of their professions. This approach underscores the importance of supportive mental health care for first responders, ensuring they have the resources they need to thrive in their challenging roles.

Police officers face the stress of upholding the law while managing unpredictable and often dangerous situations, confronting the darker aspects of human nature. Firefighters battle physical hazards and the emotional toll of witnessing life-altering events; paramedics/EMTs frequently make life-or-death decisions with lasting emotional repercussions; 911 dispatchers, as the first point of contact in emergencies, grapple with the emotional aftermath of crises they manage remotely.

This call to action emphasizes not only acknowledging the mental health challenges of first responders but also creating a culture that supports and normalizes seeking help. Destigmatizing mental health care in these professions involves institutional changes within first responder organizations and a societal shift in recognizing their emotional toll.

An effective mental health program for first responders must consider their unique stressors and traumas. Prioritizing mental health therapy, promoting openness and support is essential for building resilience in those who continue to serve with strength and endurance. Our commitment goes beyond rhetoric; it is a pledge to protect those who dedicate their lives to keeping us safe.

The Unique Challenges Faced by First Responders

First responders play an essential role in public safety but face a broad spectrum of challenges that extend beyond the physical risks of their duties. Their mental health care needs are often complex and multidimensional, stemming from being frequently placed in high-stress environments where they witness accidents, violence, and suffering, in addition to responding to natural disasters.

It would be impossible to overstate the effect of these stressful situations on first responder mental well-being. Continuous exposure to trauma can lead to severe psychological effects, extending well beyond the incidents themselves. Post-traumatic stress disorder (PTSD), anxiety, depression, and other distressing outcomes may manifest from this ongoing exposure.

First responders encounter mental health challenges unique to their line of work. Their experiences are often unpredictable and intensely distressing, necessitating specialized approaches in mental health care. Standard therapeutic methods may not adequately address the stressors associated with their roles. Recognizing and acknowledging these challenges is essential in creating effective, targeted mental health initiatives for first responders.

The stigma surrounding mental health in the first responder community adds a significant layer of complexity. The culture often values attributes like strength, resilience, and self-reliance, sometimes at the expense of seeking mental health support. Addressing this requires a comprehensive plan that includes therapeutic interventions, as well as education and advocacy within the first responder community.

Mental health challenges for first responders are intricate and demand our attention. A deep understanding of their profession is crucial, along with a tailored and empathetic approach to mental healthcare. By recognizing their specific challenges and dismantling the stigma around seeking help, we can cultivate more resilient and healthier communities of first responders.

The Role of Mental Health Therapy

Mental health therapy offers first responders crucial support in addressing their complex challenges, providing a nuanced and comprehensive approach to trauma reactions and post- traumatic stress disorder (PTSD). The role of therapy extends beyond merely alleviating symptoms; it involves gaining a deep understanding of the unique needs and experiences that characterize the demanding and often harrowing nature of first responder work.

Therapists specializing in first responders' mental health possess unique skills and insights into the multifaceted stressors these professionals encounter in emergencies. They comprehend the intense pressure, life-threatening situations, and the necessity for immediate decision-making inherent in first responders' daily lives. Through understanding these aspects, these therapists can establish therapeutic relationships based on empathy, trust, and a keen awareness of the psychological impacts of such experiences.

Personalized therapy is key to effectively addressing first responders' mental health. Therapists work closely with individuals to explore layers of trauma, facilitating introspection and healing using evidence-based approaches like cognitive-behavioral therapy (CBT) or eye movement desensitization and reprocessing (EMDR). This tailored support helps first responders manage their emotional responses to trauma, fostering resilience and emotional fortitude.

Mental health therapy for first responders goes beyond trauma processing to also include stress management. Their work's demanding nature can lead to chronic stress, which, if not addressed, may evolve into more severe mental health issues. Therapists offer coping mechanisms specifically designed for first responders, helping them handle daily challenges and lessen the overall impact of stress on their mental health.

Professional help can restore a sense of control and empowerment for first responders, offering a safe space to navigate emotions and tools to regain mastery over their mental health. Therapy not only builds resilience but also promotes a proactive approach to well-being, helping to dismantle the stigma associated with seeking help and raising mental health awareness within first responder communities.

Mental health therapy is an invaluable resource for first responders, addressing not just the immediate effects of trauma but also aiding in ongoing well-being. By recognizing their unique challenges and providing tailored therapeutic interventions, mental health professionals play a crucial role in fostering resilience, empowerment, and long-term mental health for those committed to serving and protecting others.

Addressing the Needs of Different First-Responder Niches

Addressing the individual mental health needs of different first responder groups is both necessary and complex; each profession poses its own set of unique difficulties and stresses. With so much at stake in supporting our frontline heroes' mental well-being, recognizing and addressing these needs is vital for supporting the mental well-being of our frontline heroes.

Police officers, as guardians of public safety, face the psychological strain caused by constant exposure to violence and crime. Their daily experiences, including high-stakes confrontations and witnessing the aftermath of crimes, require mental health interventions tailored for law enforcement personnel. Therapists need to understand their specific stressors to provide effective treatments for issues like PTSD, anxiety, and strained relationships within the force.

Firefighters, who regularly confront life-threatening situations and traumatic events, bear an emotional toll from rescue operations, fighting fires, and responding to accidents. This necessitates a bespoke mental health strategy, addressing the emotional impacts of these incidents and providing tools for resilience and stress management.

Paramedics and emergency medical technicians (EMTs) encounter distinct challenges, responding to serious injuries in high-pressure situations where quick decisions can be critical. Their exposure to human suffering and the urgency of their work necessitate specialized support for mental well-being. They require assistance to process trauma, manage its emotional impact, and develop coping mechanisms for long-term mental health.

Dispatchers and 911 operators, often overlooked, play a crucial role too. They manage emergency calls, relay vital information, and provide emotional support during crises. Their mental strain stems from constant alertness, handling distressful situations remotely, and dealing with unpredictable emergency calls; their specific challenges must be considered in any supportive approach.

Recognizing the individual needs of each first responder group is more than just customization; it's essential for building a comprehensive support system. By understanding the unique experiences of each first responder and incorporating this into mental health therapy, practitioners can offer tailored treatments. Such targeted therapies can address how professional demands affect personal well-being. Additionally, resilience-building programs tailored for each group can help foster an environment that promotes mental health awareness, ensuring ongoing well-being for those dedicated to public safety.

Conclusion

First responders play an invaluable role in protecting our communities, with their dedicated service providing protection and service that cannot be underestimated. Their work often involves difficult or traumatic situations, making the acknowledgment and prioritization of their mental well-being essential. While their commitment is admirable, it's equally important for first responders to recognize the importance of maintaining their mental health as they keep us safe.

Understanding the unique challenges faced by different first responder groups is key to providing effective mental health care. Sectors such as law enforcement, firefighting, and emergency medical services each have distinct stressors that can lead to trauma reactions and PTSD. Recognizing these specific needs is crucial for developing targeted therapeutic approaches, ensuring that mental health interventions are relevant and effective.

Encouraging first responders to seek professional therapy is a vital step in building a mentally healthy community. Addressing the psychological impacts of their experiences empowers them to cope more effectively with trauma. Creating a culture where seeking therapy is viewed as a strength rather than a weakness is essential, promoting an environment where professional help is part of maintaining mental well-being.

Supporting the mental well-being of first responders involves more than individual efforts; it requires a cultural shift within the communities and organizations that employ them. This shift should increase understanding of the challenges first responders face and strengthen support networks, ensuring comprehensive support for these vital community members.

Encouraging a Culture of Support and Wellness within the First Responder Community

First responders, including police officers, 911 dispatchers, fire-fighters, paramedics, and EMTs, hold critical yet demanding roles, often exposing them to traumatizing events. This can lead to mental health challenges like post-traumatic stress disorder (PTSD). It's crucial to foster a culture of support and well-being for these professionals. This exploration highlights the importance of creating a healing environment within first responder communities. It delves into the significance of this approach and the strategies required to provide mental health therapy tailored to the unique issues these professionals face.

Establish a Supportive Environment:

First-responder stress can be compounded by a lack of support, highlighting the need for a culture that values open communication, empathy, and mutual understanding among peers. Prioritizing mental health awareness and actively working to destigmatize seeking help for mental health issues are crucial steps in this process. Cultivating an environment where first responders feel both encouraged and comfortable to openly share their experiences and emotions is key. Such an atmosphere can offer significant support to those dealing with post-traumatic stress disorder (PTSD) and other mental health challenges.

Promoting Mental Health Therapy:

Mental health therapy plays a vital role in treating and managing trauma reactions and PTSD among first responders. Departments must prioritize providing access to therapy services, addressing the unique mental health needs of these individuals. Collaboration between mental health professionals, peer support programs, and confidential counseling is key to enhancing mental health therapy within the first responder community. Investing in these services equips frontline workers with the necessary tools to confidently tackle their daily challenges head-on and with confidence.

Tailoring Therapy for First Responders:

Recognizing the unique needs of first responders, mental health therapy should be specifically tailored to their experiences. Therapists must receive special training to understand the stressors and traumas inherent to first responder roles, and adapt treatment plans accordingly. This could include cognitive-behavioral therapy, eye movement desensitization and reprocessing (EMDR), or other therapeutic modalities effective in treating trauma reactions and PTSD.

Conclusions:

Promoting a culture of support and wellness among first responder communities is central to combatting the pervasive challenges posed by trauma reactions and posttraumatic stress disorder (PTSD). Prioritizing mental health services tailored to the unique needs of first responders can help build a strong support network, essential for the recovery of those who selflessly serve our communities.

Providing Resources and Tools for Mental Health Recovery

First responders face unique challenges that require special support when recovering from trauma reactions and posttraumatic stress disorder (PTSD). To best assist these first responders in coping with this aspect of their job, this subchapter explores resources specifically designed to meet their mental health needs.

Expanded Therapy Approaches:

Cognitive-Behavioral Therapy (CBT):

When it comes to evidence-based therapies, cognitive-behavioral therapy (CBT) stands out as a cornerstone approach. CBT moves beyond superficial discussions by delving deep into negative thought patterns and behaviors linked to trauma. CBT not only facilitates an understanding of these but provides first responders with effective coping strategies and skills necessary for navigating distressful symptoms effectively. The emphasis here is not simply on past trauma but on supporting individuals' present and future mental well-being.

Eye Movement Desensitization and Reprocessing (EMDR):

Custom-tailored for trauma victims, Eye Movement Desensitization and Reprocessing (EMDR) employs bilateral stimulation to reprocess traumatic memories, reducing their emotional impact and aiding in mental health restoration. This innovative approach acknowledges the effects of trauma on both mind and body, providing transformative techniques that empower first responders to regain control over their emotional reactions.

Trauma-Focused Cognitive Behavioral Therapy (TF-CBT):

Created specifically with post-traumatic stress disorder in mind, trauma-focused cognitive behavioral therapy (TF-CBT) blends cognitive behavioral therapy principles with trauma specific strategies. This method gives first responders a tailored therapy that suits their unique needs, addressing the complex trauma they face in service. TF-CBT provides a nuanced approach to healing by focusing on cognitive restructuring and including trauma-specific interventions during therapy sessions.

Enhance Peer Support Programs:

While peer support programs have long been recognized, their true strength lies in providing first responders a haven to share experiences and receive advice from others who have undergone similar trauma. Peer groups offer not just support networks but an intimately understood community where emotional support becomes something shared rather than simply serviced as needed.

Advanced Online Resources:

Online resources have become increasingly important for mental health recovery, with platforms like NAMI, Mental Health America, and SAMHSA offering not only information but also interactive tools and virtual support groups. These digital spaces allow first responders to participate in discussions, webinars, and forums, gaining valuable insights and perspectives from a wider community.

Innovative Mobile Apps:

The integration of technology into mental health support has led to the development of innovative mobile apps tailored to mental health recovery. From guided meditation and mindfulness apps to real-time stress management tools, these applications are designed to be accessible at any time, accommodating the unpredictable schedules of first responders.

Organizations are increasingly embracing comprehensive workplace wellness programs in response to the unique challenges faced by first responders, acknowledging the special considerations their roles demand. These programs extend beyond mere awareness campaigns to include workshops and training sessions that delve into mental health issues in depth. Incorporating mental health professionals into these initiatives not only emphasizes emotional well-being but also demonstrates a commitment to an open workplace culture with supportive management that values and understands its employees. Furthermore, these programs are designed not just to react to mental health crises but to proactively equip first responders with the tools they need for ongoing resilience, something awareness campaigns alone cannot achieve.

As mental health recovery resources and tools for first responders become more sophisticated and evolve, so do their support systems. From advanced therapeutic approaches to digital innovations, the focus remains on creating an all-encompassing support system that recognizes and addresses the unique challenges faced by emergency responders. By further exploring these resources, the goal is to not only acknowledge the struggles faced by first responders but also to provide a roadmap towards resilient recovery, ensuring mental well-being remains a top priority.

First responders often face trauma-induced reactions and post-traumatic stress disorder (PTSD), leading to mental health challenges that need to be recognized and managed appropriately. Seeking help is not a sign of weakness but a demonstration of strength and resilience; starting the journey to mental health recovery requires acknowledging their needs and utilizing the available tools that support the recovery process.

Mental health specialists play a pivotal role in providing tailored therapies specifically designed for first responder experiences. These experts have the expertise to help individuals navigate through trauma and PTSD symptoms, creating a safe environment for expression and healing. Therapy is a key element of the recovery process, providing coping strategies, emotional support, and structured methods for addressing recovery challenges.

Beyond traditional therapy, there exists a wealth of resources and tools are available to help individuals manage their mental well-being. Educational materials, online platforms, and mobile apps offer practical solutions for managing stress, anxiety, and other mental health issues, acting as supplements to therapy sessions and fostering resilience and self-awareness.

Peer support networks play an invaluable role in mental health recovery. Sharing similar experiences with fellow first responders fosters camaraderie and understanding, helping the healing process along. Peer support groups, both formal and informal, provide spaces for sharing experiences, exchanging coping techniques, and cultivating a community of mutual support throughout the recovery journey.

Technology plays a central role in expanding access to mental health resources in today's digital world. Teletherapy services allow first responders to connect with mental health professionals remotely, offering greater flexibility and access, especially for those in remote areas or with demanding schedules. Mobile apps dedicated to mental health give individuals tools for relaxation, mindfulness, and stress management right at their fingertips, fostering consistent self-care practices.

Research and development are essential in advancing mental health resources and tools. Investment in new technologies, therapeutic methods, and support programs ensures that individuals have access to the latest interventions and contributes to an ongoing improvement in mental health care for first responders.

Recognizing the courage required to seek help is the first step towards mental health recovery. Engaging with a range of resources and tools offers a comprehensive path towards healing, empowerment, and regaining mental well-being. Integrating specialized therapy, peer support, digital innovations, and continuous research creates a strong framework to meet the unique challenges faced by first responders in restoring their mental health.

About The Author

Dennis J. Carradin, Jr.

Dennis is a Licensed Professional Counselor of Mental Health, a Nationally Certified Counselor, a Board-Certified Expert in Traumatic Stress, and a Diplomate for the American Academy of Experts in Traumatic Stress.

Currently, he is the Executive Director of New Perspectives, Inc., a private counseling agency in Delaware, and served on the faculty of Penn State University, Brandywine Campus, for 15 years. He is a Vice President and Principal Consultant for SSC Consulting. Dennis is a trained trainer for R-3 Continuum. He is the President and CEO of the Trauma Survivors Foundation. He serves on three international trauma firms.

Dennis is a former Nationally Registered Emergency Medical Technician and a former Emergency Medical Technician with the state of Delaware. He is a former volunteer firefighter. Dennis serves as a LAST member for the National Fallen Firefighter Foundation in conjunction with the National Fire Academy. He is the clinical director and team coordinator of the New Castle, Kent, and Sussex County CISM teams as well as the Wilmington Police and New Castle County Police CISM teams, the AI DuPont CISM team, and the State of Delaware CISM team. Dennis is the State CISM Chairman for the Delaware Volunteer Fireman's Association. He is the President of the Wilmington West Rotary Club. He is listed in the National Center for Crisis Management's directory of expert witnesses and premiere speaker's bureau.

He has attended Millersville University, Temple University, and Walden University. Dennis has conducted numerous debriefings on domestic as well as international disasters, shootings, bombings, bank robberies, corporate incidents, school disasters, and Fire, EMS, and Police tragedies including, but not limited to, the attacks on the WTC in NYC, the Hurricane Katrina and Hurricane Sandy relief efforts, the Sandy Hook Elementary School Shootings, the Boston Marathon Bombings, the DC Navy Yard shootings, the Paramus Park mall shootings, the Pulse Night Club shooting, the Hurricane Harvey Relief efforts, the Annapolis shootings, Las Vegas shootings, and the Capitol Building Insurrection.

www.ingramcontent.com/pod-product-compliance
Lightning Source LLC
Chambersburg PA
CBHW060923140726
47996CB00001B/350